AUTHORS

Jacqueline Chanda
Kristen Pederson Marstaller

CONSULTANTS

Katherina Danko-McGhee
María Teresa García-Pedroche

SCHOOL PUBLISHERS

Orlando   Austin   New York   San Diego   Toronto   London

Visit *The Learning Site!*
www.harcourtschool.com

Printed in the United States of America

ISBN 0-15-336448-3

2 3 4 5 6 7 8 9 10   048   13 12 11 10 09 08 07 06 05

Dear Young Artist,

Art can be made from many different things. In this book, you will see artworks made from paints, clay, yarn—even old baseballs! What kinds of things do you use to make art?

The artworks in this book come from many places around the world. Artists often get ideas from their communities.

As you create your own artworks, look around your community. Your next art idea may be right in front of you!

Sincerely,
The Authors

CONTENTS

Unit 1   Inside and Out 22
Line, Shape, and Form

4

Unit 2 The Artist's Plan 42
Color, Value, and Texture

Unit 3 Tell Your Story 62

Proportion, Movement, and Pattern

Unit 4 Special Places 82

Space and Emphasis

Unit 5 Surprising Viewpoints ...102
Balance and Unity

AT A GLANCE

Art Production

Elements and Principles

Cross-Curricular Connections

Media

Keeping a
Sketchbook

A sketch is a rough drawing that shows an idea for an artwork. You can keep sketches together in a sketchbook. Make sketches of things you imagine and things you see.

Thomas Locker is an artist who enjoys nature. He plans his artworks by making sketches of different places in nature. Then he uses the sketches to create paintings.

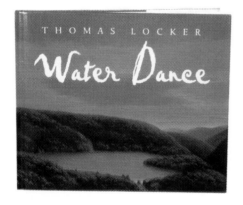

Locker is also an author. He writes words to go with his paintings. The paintings and words are made into books.

Use a sketchbook to plan your own artworks.
Next to your drawings, write notes about colors
or materials you might use.

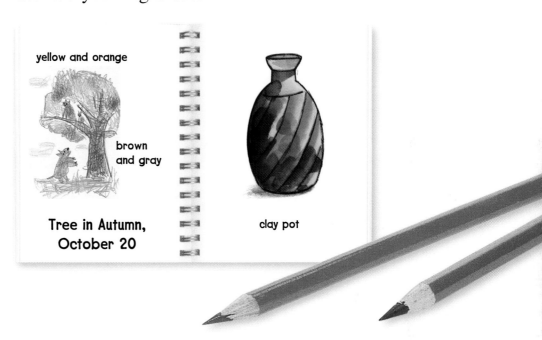

yellow and orange

brown
and gray

Tree in Autumn,
October 20

clay pot

Collect pictures and other things in your
sketchbook. Look at your sketchbook to
get ideas for your art.

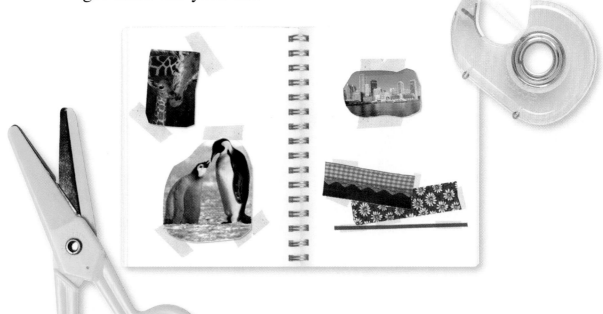

Visiting a Museum

An art museum is a place where artworks are collected and displayed. You can find art museums in cities and towns all over the world.

When you visit a museum, remember to

- **Walk** slowly and quietly. Note the artworks that catch your eye.

- **Look** closely at the artworks, but don't touch them.

- **Think** about what the artist's message might be.

- **Listen** carefully to what the docent, or guide, tells you about the artworks.

- **Speak** quietly, but don't be afraid to ask questions.

▲ High Museum of Art
Atlanta, Georgia

◀ The Museum of Fine Arts, Houston
Houston, Texas

Fast Fact More than 45,000 artworks are displayed in this museum. It is one of the largest museums in the United States.

Looking at Art

You may see artworks in museums, in books, or on websites. When you look at an artwork, you can follow these steps to better understand what you see:

- **DESCRIBE**   Look closely at the artwork. How would you describe it to someone who has not seen it?

- **ANALYZE**   Think about the way the artist organized the artwork. When you glance at it quickly, what catches your eye first?

- **INTERPRET**   What do you think the artist's message is? Sometimes the title of an artwork can give you a clue.

- **EVALUATE**   What is your opinion of the artwork? Think about why you do or do not like it. Do you think the artist was successful?

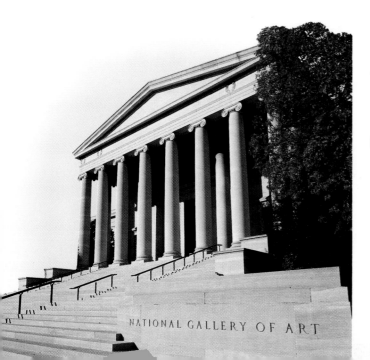

◀ **National Gallery of Art**
Washington, D.C.

Fast Fact The two buildings of this museum are connected by an underground walkway. The museum also features an outdoor sculpture garden.

NATIONAL GALLERY OF ART

Reading Your Textbook

Knowing how to read your art textbook will help you remember and enjoy what you read. Each lesson contains nonfiction text about artists, artworks, art techniques, and art history. Remember that nonfiction texts give facts about real people, things, events, or places.

The **title** tells the main topic of the lesson.

Highlighted words are art **vocabulary**.

You can identify the most important ideas in each lesson by becoming familiar with different features of your textbook. Look at this sample lesson from pages 52–53.

Lesson 8

Vocabulary

value

shades

tints

Color and Mood

Imagine a room with blue walls, blue furniture, and blue carpeting. Would the room give you a calm feeling or an excited feeling? Artists use color to create a certain mood, or feeling. What kind of mood do you feel when you look at the painting below?

Look for lighter and darker yellow in the painting. The lightness or darkness of a color is its **value**. Artists mix black paint with a color to make **shades**. They mix white paint with a color to make **tints**. Point out some shades and tints of green in the painting.

Diego Rivera,
Baile en Tehuantepec

You can find more resources in the Student Handbook:

- Maps of Museums and Art Sites, pp. 144–147

- Art Safety, pp. 148–149

- Art Techniques, pp. 150–165

- Elements and Principles, pp. 166–177

- Gallery of Artists, pp. 178–188

- Glossary, pp. 189–197

Artist's Workshop

Mood Painting

PLAN

Think of a special event such as a party. Sketch a scene from the event. Think about the mood you want to create in a painting of the scene.

CREATE

1. Draw the scene on white paper.

2. Choose colors that will create the mood you want to show. Mix tints and shades of those colors.

3. Paint the scene.

REFLECT

Look at your finished painting. How did you use color to create a mood? Where did you use tints and shades?

Quick Tip

To mix tints, add white paint to a color.

  + =

To mix shades, add black paint to a color.

 + =

The Artist's Workshop activities are organized by the steps Plan, Create, and Reflect.

The photographs on this page show how an artwork can be made.

These are important tips about art techniques or safety.

53

Elements and Principles

Elements of Art

The **elements of art** are the basic parts of an artwork. You can use them to describe art and to plan and create your own artworks. As you look at these photographs, think about other places where you have seen the elements of art.

COLOR ▲

what we see when light is reflected off objects

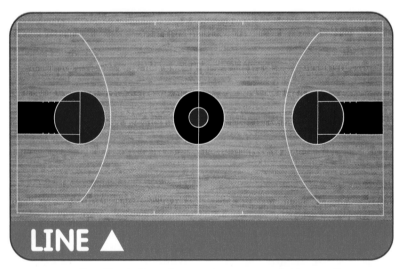

LINE ▲

a mark that begins at one point and continues for a certain distance

FORM ▲

an object that has height, width, and depth

See also Elements and Principles, pages 166–177.

SPACE ▲

the area between and around objects

SHAPE ▲

an object that has height and width

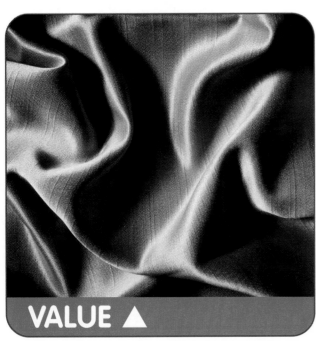

VALUE ▲

the lightness or darkness of a color

TEXTURE ▲

the way a surface looks or feels

Principles of Design

Artists use the **principles of design** to arrange the elements in an artwork. Look at how the elements of art are arranged in these photographs.

PATTERN ▲

a design made with repeating lines, shapes, or colors

PROPORTION ▲

the size of one thing compared with another thing

BALANCE ▲

the arrangement of elements on each side of an artwork

VARIETY ▲

the use of different elements in an artwork

See also Elements and Principles, pages 166–177.

EMPHASIS ▲

importance given to a certain part of an artwork

MOVEMENT ▲

the path your eyes take around an artwork

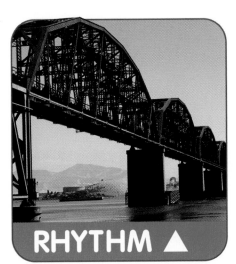

RHYTHM ▲

the use of repeating elements to create a visual beat

UNITY ▲

the sense that an artwork looks complete and that its parts go together

Henri Matisse, *Harmony in Red*

LOCATE IT

This painting can be found at the Hermitage Museum in St. Petersburg, Russia.

See Maps of Museums and Art Sites, pages 144–147.

St. Petersburg

RUSSIA

Inside and Out

Inside, Outside

Inside is a big, grand room.
Outside flowers are in bloom.

Inside it is quiet and still.
Outside sparrows chirp and trill.

Inside tables will be set,
but outside we are playing yet.

Anonymous

Unit Vocabulary

lines	organic shapes
contour lines	still life
landscape	composition
jagged lines	three-dimensional
two-dimensional	forms
geometric shapes	sculpture

ABOUT THE ARTIST

See Gallery of Artists, pages 178–188.

Multimedia Art Glossary
Visit *The Learning Site*
www.harcourtschool.com

Draw Conclusions

Sometimes you need to use clues to understand what you see. You *draw conclusions* when you think about what you see and about what you already know.

Look at the image below. You can draw the conclusion that the women are watching something funny by using these clues:

- **What You See** The woman in the back is covering her mouth, and the woman in the front is smiling.

- **What You Already Know** People sometimes cover their mouths when they are laughing. People smile when they see something funny.

Bartolomé Esteban Murillo,
Two Women at a Window

You can also draw conclusions to help you understand what you read. Read the passage below. Use what you read and what you already know to draw conclusions.

Bartolomé Esteban Murillo (moo•REE•yoh) was born in 1618. He was the first artist from Spain to become famous worldwide. Murillo made many paintings of people on the streets of Spain. He also made paintings for churches. In Spain today, a fine painting by any artist is often called a *Murillo.*

Do you think Murillo is still famous in Spain? Why or why not? Use a diagram like this to draw conclusions.

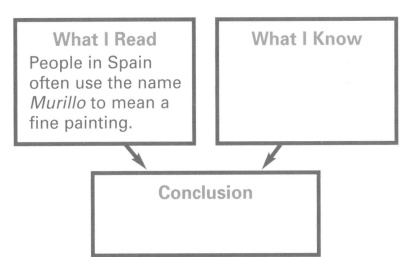

What I Read
People in Spain often use the name *Murillo* to mean a fine painting.

What I Know

Conclusion

On Your Own

As you read the lessons in this unit, use diagrams like the one above to draw conclusions about the text and the artworks.

Kinds of Lines

Look at the different kinds of **lines** on page 27, and find some of these lines in the objects around you. You may find lines on the pages of a notebook. You may also see lines that reach from the floor to the top of a door. What other kinds of lines do you see?

In the painting below, find lines that are straight, curved, and zigzag. What other kinds of lines do you see?

Henri Matisse,
Interior in Yellow and Blue

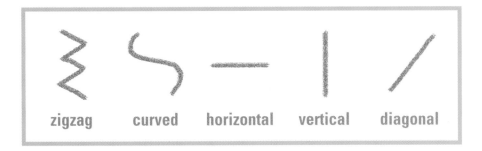

| zigzag | curved | horizontal | vertical | diagonal |

Lines that outline objects are called **contour lines**. Point out some objects in the painting on page 26 that have contour lines.

Artist's Workshop

Crayon Etching

1. **Use colored pencils to draw thick stripes on white paper. Cover all of the paper.**

2. **Use black crayon to color over the stripes. Cover all of the paper.**

3. **Think about a line design you would like to make.**

4. **Use a paper clip to scratch the design through the black crayon. The colors will show through in your design.**

Lines Express Feelings

The image below is a **landscape**, or outdoor scene. Read the title of the painting. What feeling about the Wild West do you think the artist wanted to show?

Emil Armin,
Wild West

Artists can use lines to show how they feel about something. In the painting above, the artist used thick, **jagged lines** to create an exciting feeling. The jagged lines also show that the land is rough and bumpy. How would the painting be different if the artist had used many straight lines? What feeling do you think gently curving lines would create?

Artist's Workshop

Expressive Line Drawing

Choose an outdoor scene you would like to draw. Then think about the feelings you would like to express. What kinds of lines will you use? Sketch some ideas.

1. Copy your best sketch onto white paper.

2. Add details to the landscape. Include different lines that show your feelings about the scene.

3. Use colored pencils to finish the drawing.

What kinds of lines did you use in your drawing? How do the lines show your feelings about the scene?

Quick Tip

These lines can show different feelings. You may want to use some of them in your drawing.

curved
calm

zigzag
powerful

jagged
exciting

vertical
strong

29

Wassily Kan

Why do artists paint pictures that do not show real objects?

In 1895, Wassily Kandinsky (vuh•SEEL•yee kan•DIN•skee) saw an artwork that confused him. He could not figure out what the artist had painted. At the time, Kandinsky thought artists should make their artworks look almost like photographs. His first paintings had shown real objects — houses and outdoor scenes. Look at images **A** and **B**. How do you think Kandinsky's ideas about art changed?

Kandinsky saw ways in which art and music are alike. He used lines, shapes, and colors to express feelings the way instruments do in music. What feeling does image **A** express?

A **Wassily Kandinsky,**
Yellow-Red-Blue

dinsky

Kandinsky's style of painting became very popular with artists who wanted to try something new. These artists were called Expressionists because they used art to express feelings.

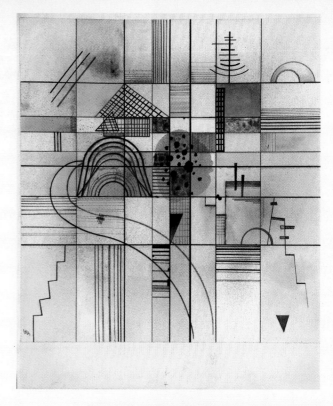

 Wassily Kandinsky, *Varied Rectangle (Variierte Rechtecke)*

Wassily Kandinsky's studio

Think About Art

Think of a song that you enjoy. If you were to paint while listening to the song, what would your painting look like? What kinds of lines would you use?

 **Multimedia Biographies**
Visit *The Learning Site*
www.harcourtschool.com

31

Lesson
3

Vocabulary

two-dimensional

geometric
shapes

organic shapes

Geometric and Organic Shapes

Shapes are **two-dimensional**, or flat. You can measure the height and width of a shape.

Artists use lines to make shapes. **Geometric shapes** such as squares, rectangles, and triangles can be drawn with straight lines. Circles and ovals are geometric shapes that have curved edges. What geometric shapes do you see in this artwork?

Organic shapes are found in nature. They show things such as flowers and can be drawn with wavy lines and irregular borders. Find some organic shapes in the artwork. What objects from nature do they show?

Unknown artist,
Brazilian Tapestry
(Six Patterns)

Artist's Workshop

Shape Design

PLAN ·

Sketch a design made up of geometric and organic shapes. Draw smaller shapes inside larger shapes.

CREATE ·

1. Copy the shapes from your sketch onto colored construction paper.

2. Cut out the shapes.

3. Use your sketch as a guide to place the shapes. Then glue them onto black paper.

REFLECT ·

Look at your design. Describe the organic shapes. What kinds of geometric shapes did you use?

Quick Tip

Trace classroom objects or use a ruler to draw geometric shapes. You might trace the top of a cup to draw a circle.

Lesson 4

Vocabulary

still life

composition

Shapes in Still Lifes

A **still life** is an artwork that shows a group of objects. Everyday objects are often the subjects of still lifes.

To create a still life, an artist arranges geometric and organic shapes into an interesting composition. A **composition** is the way an artist puts together lines, shapes, and colors in an artwork. What geometric and organic shapes do you see in image **A**? How would you describe this still life?

Image **B** is also a still life. Describe the composition the artist used. Now look at the still life in image **C**, and point out the geometric and organic shapes you see.

A Fernando Botero, *Fruit*

William H. Johnson,
Flowers

Lauren,
grade 3,
*Autumn
Still Life*

Artist's Workshop

Still-Life Painting

1. **On a desk or table, arrange some objects that have different shapes and sizes. Create an interesting composition.**

2. **Sketch your still life by drawing the geometric and organic shapes you see.**

3. **Paint your still life.**

Art and Geometry

Why is math important to artists?

Math has always been an important tool for artists. Shapes that are used in math can be found in almost every artwork. Look at the cat in image **A**. It was made almost completely with triangles. Does the cat look as soft and smooth as a real cat? Why or why not?

 Diana Ong, *Kat*

Image **B** shows an artwork that is not made up of flat shapes. The artwork can be viewed from different sides. Which part of it looks like a ball? Do the other parts look like objects you recognize?

DID YOU KNOW?

The artist of image **A** did not use paints or pencils. She created the image with a computer. In the past, artists had to use numbers to tell computers where to place lines and colors. Now artists can draw computer images more easily with a mouse.

Think
About Art

Think of an animal you would like to draw. What geometric shapes could you use?

B Dame Barbara Hepworth, *Three Forms*

Geometric and Organic Forms

Objects that are **three-dimensional** have height, width, and depth. They are called **forms**. Which of these geometric forms do you see around you?

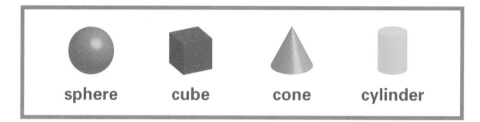

sphere   cube   cone   cylinder

A **sculpture** is a three-dimensional artwork. Look at the sculpture in image **A**. What geometric forms did the artist use to show a person's head and body?

Image **B** shows an organic form. Organic forms are like the forms you see in nature. What object in nature does this form look like?

A Alexander Archipenko, *Carrousel Pierrot*

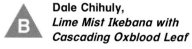

B Dale Chihuly, *Lime Mist Ikebana with Cascading Oxblood Leaf*

Artist's Workshop

Organic Form Sculpture

PLAN ·

Look at natural objects to get ideas for your sculpture. Sketch some ideas.

CREATE ·

1. To get air bubbles out, put the clay on a paper bag and press down on it. Then fold the clay over and press down again.

2. Sculpt an organic form by pinching and pulling the clay.

3. Use carving tools to add details to your sculpture.

4. Let your sculpture dry completely.

REFLECT ·

Describe the organic form you created. What object in nature does it look like?

 Quick Tip You can join two pieces of clay together by carving lines into both pieces. Then wet the pieces and press them together.

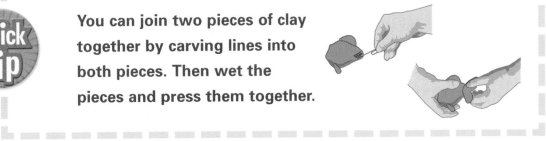

Unit 1 Review and Reflect

Choose the letter of the word or phrase that best completes each sentence.

1 Artists use ___ lines to outline objects.

    A curved   **C** wavy

    B zigzag   **D** contour

2 A ___ is a picture of an outdoor scene.

    A still life   **C** landscape

    B composition   **D** sculpture

3 A painting that shows a group of objects is a ___.

    A sculpture   **C** landscape

    B still life   **D** design

4 Shapes like those in nature are called ___.

    A landscapes   **C** forms

    B geometric shapes   **D** organic shapes

5 Shapes are flat, but forms are ___.

    A two-dimensional   **C** three-dimensional

    B curved   **D** straight

READING SKILL

Draw Conclusions

Reread pages 30–31. Use what you read and what you know to draw conclusions about Wassily Kandinsky's style of art. Use a diagram like the one shown here.

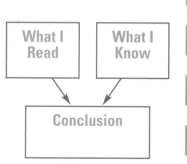

Write About Art

Choose an artwork from this unit. Then write a paragraph in which you draw conclusions about the artwork. Use a diagram to plan your writing.

REMEMBER—YOU SHOULD

- write about what you see and about what you already know.

- use correct grammar, spelling, and punctuation.

Critic's Corner

Look at *Prades, the Village* by Joan Miró (hoh•AHN mee•ROH) to answer the questions below.

DESCRIBE   What do you see in the painting?

ANALYZE   What kinds of lines did the artist use? Where do you see geometric and organic shapes?

INTERPRET   What feeling do the lines express?

EVALUATE   What do you think of the way the artist used lines and shapes to express a feeling? Explain your answer.

Joan Miró, *Prades, the Village*

Claes Oldenburg and Coosje van Bruggen, *Torn Notebook*

LOCATE IT

This sculpture can be found in Lincoln, Nebraska.

See Maps of Museums and Art Sites, pages 144–147.

NEBRASKA

Lincoln

The Artist's Plan

Wind Tricks

The wind is full of tricks today,

He blew my daddy's hat away.

He chased our paper down the street.

He almost blew us off our feet.

He makes the trees and bushes dance.

Just listen to him howl and prance.

Anonymous

ABOUT THE ARTISTS

See Gallery of Artists, pages 178–188.

Unit Vocabulary

primary colors	shades
secondary colors	tints
intermediate colors	tactile texture
warm colors	weaving
cool colors	photorealism
value	visual texture

Multimedia Art Glossary
Visit *The Learning Site*
www.harcourtschool.com

Main Idea

The *main idea* tells what something is mostly about. Details can help support the main idea.

The main idea of the painting below is that a train called the Ole '97 suddenly jumped off the tracks. You can tell this is the main idea by looking at these supporting details:

- what the title of the painting means

- why the people in the painting look surprised

- how the train tracks look

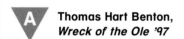

A   **Thomas Hart Benton,**
Wreck of the Ole '97

As you read, think about what the text is mostly about. This will help you understand what you are reading. Read the passage below. Look for details that support the main idea.

Thomas Hart Benton made paintings of scenes from American life. Benton got many of his ideas for paintings from the lives of farmers and railroad workers. He got other ideas from songs. He traveled around the country, making sketches of people living their lives. *Wreck of the Ole '97* is one of Benton's paintings. It is based on something that really happened.

What is this passage mostly about? What are some details in the passage? Use a diagram like this to help you.

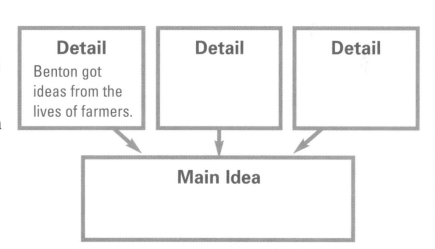

Detail	Detail	Detail
Benton got ideas from the lives of farmers.		

Main Idea

On Your Own

As you read the lessons in this unit, use diagrams like the one above to write about main ideas and details in the text and the artworks.

The Color Wheel

Artists may use a color wheel to help them plan artworks. Look at the color wheel on page 47. Find the colors red, blue, and yellow. These are the **primary colors**. They can be mixed to make any other color on the color wheel. Now look at the painting below. Where do you see primary colors in this painting?

Robert Delaunay,
Woman pouring, Portuguese still life

Secondary colors are made by mixing two primary colors together. Orange, violet, and green are secondary colors. Find them on the color wheel. Red and yellow mixed together make orange. Which two primary colors mixed together make violet? What about green? Point out the secondary colors in the painting.

Now find blue and violet on the color wheel. The color between them is blue-violet. **Intermediate colors** are made by mixing a primary color with a secondary color that is next to it on the color wheel. Name the other intermediate colors on the color wheel.

Artist's Workshop

Indoor Scene Painting

1. **Use a pencil to draw a scene from a room you know well.**

2. **Decide what colors of paint you will use. Look at the color wheel above to help you mix your colors.**

3. **Paint the scene.**

Color Groups

Look at images **A** and **B**. What kind of weather do you see in these paintings? What colors did the artist use in image **A**?

Artists often use colors such as red, orange, and yellow to show warm places. Red, orange, and yellow are **warm colors**. Find them on the color wheel on page 47. In image **A** the artist used mostly warm colors to create the hot feeling of a desert.

A Georgia O'Keeffe,
My Back Yard

Cool colors are found opposite warm colors on the color wheel. Green, blue, and violet are cool colors. For the painting in image **B**, the artist used mostly cool colors to show a cold day. What other details in the painting tell you it is a winter scene? Where do you see warm colors in image **B**? Why do you think the artist used them?

 Josephine Trotter,
Winter Palace

Artist's Workshop

Seasonal Drawing

1. **Think of an outdoor scene in summer or winter. Draw it on white paper.**

2. **Use either warm colors or cool colors to show weather in your scene.**

3. **Add details to your drawing that help show the kind of weather.**

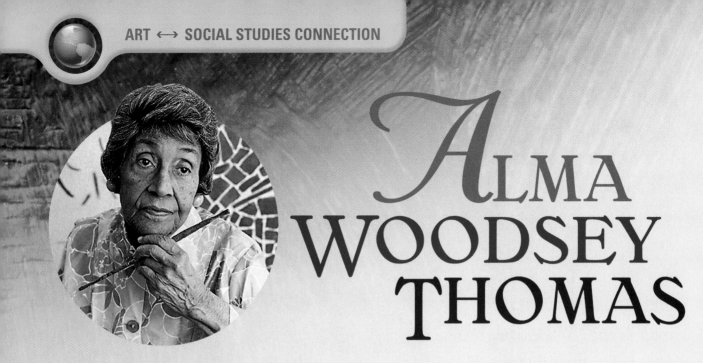

ALMA WOODSEY THOMAS

How do artists get ideas for their artworks?

Alma Woodsey Thomas was an artist for most of her life. As a child, she used clay from a river near her home to make sculptures. Her memories of the flowers outside her home became part of her paintings many years later.

Thomas saw nature in a special way. From her window, she watched patches of color change with the seasons. In her paintings, she used patches of color, too. She sometimes used them to show how the ground might look from an airplane. Look at the shapes and colors in image A. What season do you think they show?

Alma Woodsey Thomas,
Fall Begins

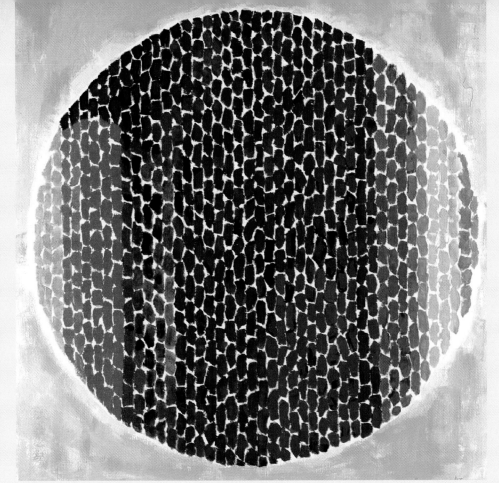

Thomas also used art to show her interest in space. Look at the title of image **B**. *Snoopy* was the nickname for a real spacecraft. Thomas imagined what the astronauts saw looking out from space. What do you see in image **B**?

THINK ABOUT ART

What would you like to paint from a spacecraft view? What colors would you use?

DID YOU KNOW?

Snoopy was part of the *Apollo 10* space mission in 1969. The astronauts on the mission went closer to the moon than anyone had been before. They took pictures to help other astronauts get ready for a moon landing later that year.

GO ONLINE

Multimedia Biographies
Visit *The Learning Site*
www.harcourtschool.com

Color and Mood

Imagine a room with blue walls, blue furniture, and blue carpeting. Would the room give you a calm feeling or an excited feeling? Artists use color to create a certain mood, or feeling. What kind of mood do you feel when you look at the painting below?

Look for lighter and darker yellow in the painting. The lightness or darkness of a color is its **value**. Artists mix black paint with a color to make **shades**. They mix white paint with a color to make **tints**. Point out some shades and tints of green in the painting.

Diego Rivera,
Baile en Tehuantepec

Diego Rivera

Artist's Workshop

Mood Painting

PLAN

Think of a special event such as a party. Sketch a scene from the event. Think about the mood you want to create in a painting of the scene.

CREATE

1. Draw the scene on white paper.

2. Choose colors that will create the mood you want to show. Mix tints and shades of those colors.

3. Paint the scene.

REFLECT

Look at your finished painting. How did you use color to create a mood? Where did you use tints and shades?

Quick Tip

To mix tints, add white paint to a color.

To mix shades, add black paint to a color.

Tactile Texture

Have you ever felt the fuzzy skin of a peach or the smooth skin of an apple? **Tactile texture** is the way an object feels when you touch it. Touch some of the things around you. Describe the textures you feel.

Tactile texture can make an artwork more interesting or surprising. Look at image **A**. What do you see? The artist covered smooth objects with a surprising texture. What do you think the artwork feels like?

Image **B** is a **weaving** made of yarn. Rugs and baskets are also kinds of weavings. What do you think image **B** feels like?

B Hailey, age 8, Weaving

A Meret Oppenheim, *Object*

Artist's Workshop

Texture Weaving

PLAN ....

Think about the kind of texture you want in your weaving. Choose materials with textures and colors that you like.

CREATE ....

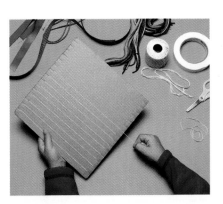

1. Cut fifteen ½-inch slits along the top and bottom of a cardboard square. Try to put equal space between each slit.

2. Wrap string through each slit around the cardboard. Tape the ends of the string to the back of the cardboard.

3. Weave the yarn and the ribbon over and under the string to create your weaving. Tie the ends in a knot on the back of the cardboard.

REFLECT ....

How would you describe the texture in your weaving?

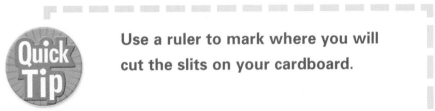

Quick Tip

Use a ruler to mark where you will cut the slits on your cardboard.

Traditions in Dance

How do artists show community pride?

Artists often tell about things that are important in their communities. Dance is one kind of art that people use to show community pride. Dancers use movement and their clothing to send a message.

The dancers in image **A** are at a Native American gathering called a powwow. Native American dance often tells a story about nature.

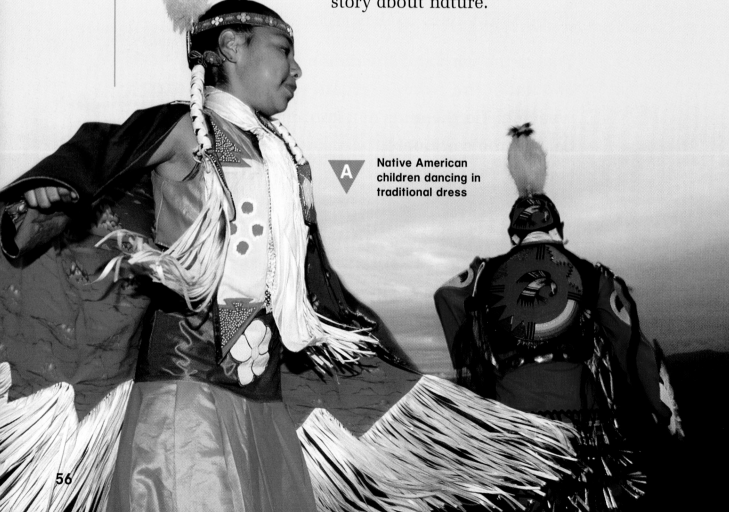

A Native American children dancing in traditional dress

56

 Traditional dancers in Korea

Image **B** shows a group of dancers in Korea. They are using objects and simple hand movements to tell stories from their culture. What do you notice about the dancers' clothing in image **B**?

Think About Art

What kind of clothing would you wear for a dance about your community? What kind of music would you use?

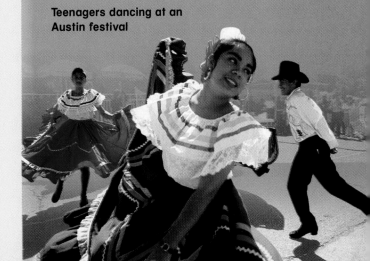

Visual Texture

Look at image **A**. Does it show a photograph or a painting? Image **A** is an example of **photorealism**. Paintings in this style look almost like photographs.

How would you describe the tactile texture of real marbles? The artist of image **A** painted the marbles to look smooth. He gave them visual texture. **Visual texture** shows the way a real object would feel if you touched it. What color did the artist use to show light shining on the tops of the marbles?

A Charles Bell,
Dazzling Dozen

Compare the visual textures of the baskets in image **B** and the marbles in image **A**. Notice how the artist of the painting in image **B** used many tiny lines to create the visual texture of grass. What other objects in image **B** have visual texture?

Artist's Workshop

Texture Rubbings

1. **Find some objects with different textures. Cover each object with tracing paper. Rub peeled crayons on the paper to show the objects' textures.**

2. **Draw some organic or geometric shapes on the rubbings. Cut out the shapes.**

3. **Arrange the shapes on construction paper in an interesting way. Glue the shapes to the paper.**

4. **Paint the rubbings with watercolors.**

Unit 2   Review and Reflect

Choose the letter of the word or phrase that best completes each sentence.

1 Artists mix white paint with a color to make ___.

   A tints   **C** moods

   B shades   **D** textures

2 Artists make ___ colors by mixing a primary color with a secondary color.

   A intermediate   **C** warm

   B lighter   **D** cool

3 Artists often use ___ colors to show cold weather.

   A warm   **C** secondary

   B cool   **D** darker

4 ___ colors can be mixed to make all the other colors on the color wheel.

   A Warm   **C** Primary

   B Cool   **D** Secondary

5 ___ is the way an object feels when you touch it.

   A Visual   **C** Tactile
       texture   texture

   B Photorealism **D** Value

READING SKILL

Main Idea

Reread the first paragraph on page 47. Write details and the main idea in a diagram like the one shown here.

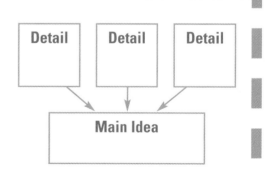

Write About Art

Write a paragraph that tells the main idea in one of your own artworks. Include the title of the artwork in your paragraph. Use a diagram to plan your writing.

REMEMBER—YOU SHOULD

- write about the main idea.

- use details that support the main idea.

- use correct grammar, spelling, and punctuation.

Critic's Corner

Look at *Ice and Clouds* by Arthur G. Dove to answer the questions below.

DESCRIBE What do you see in the painting?

ANALYZE What colors did the artist use? Where do you see tints and shades of blue?

INTERPRET What kind of mood did the artist of this painting create?

EVALUATE Do you like the way the artist used color to show a mood? Why or why not?

Arthur G. Dove, *Ice and Clouds*

Pierre-Auguste Renoir, *Afternoon of the Children at Wargemont*

LOCATE IT

This painting can be found at the New National Gallery in Berlin, Germany.

See Maps of Museums and Art Sites, pages 144–147.

Berlin

GERMANY

Tell Your Story

A Book

Closed, I am a mystery.

Open, I will always be

a friend with whom you think and see.

Closed, there's nothing I can say.

Open, we can dream and stray

to other worlds, far and away.

Myra Cohn Livingston

Unit Vocabulary

portrait   patterns
proportion   symmetry
self-portrait   mola
seascape   mural
movement

ABOUT THE ARTIST

See Gallery of Artists, pages 178–188.

Multimedia Art Glossary
Visit *The Learning Site*
www.harcourtschool.com

Narrative Elements

Narrative elements are the parts of a story. They include characters, setting, and plot. *Characters* are the people or animals. The *setting* is where and when a story takes place. The *plot* is what happens.

Artists may also tell stories in their artworks. Look at the narrative elements in the image below.

- The **characters** are a coyote, an eagle, a bear, rabbits, and many other animals.

- The **setting** is a canyon at night.

- The **plot** seems to be that the coyote is telling the other animals something important.

**Harriet Peck Taylor, Illustration
from *Coyote Places the Stars*** LITERATURE LINK

Thinking about the characters, setting, and plot can help you understand the stories you read. Read the story below.

"Are we almost there?" María asked her parents from the back seat of the car.

María always looked forward to family vacations. She had helped plan this trip to Big Bend National Park by researching things to do there. Along with her clothes, María had packed her sketchbook. She wanted to draw the plants and animals she would see. When the car finally stopped, María was filled with excitement.

"Let's go exploring!" she shouted.

Who are the characters in the story, and where are they? What are the characters doing? Use a story map like this to describe the characters, setting, and plot of the story.

Characters	Setting
María, María's parents	

Plot (Story Events)
1.
2.
3.

On Your Own

As you look at the artworks in this unit, think about the stories the artists are trying to tell. Use story maps to write about what you see.

Portraits

A **portrait** is a picture of a person. Artists can use proportion to make portraits look lifelike. **Proportion** is the size and placement of some things compared with other things. Look at the portrait in image **A**. Notice that the girl's eyes are halfway between her chin and the top of her head. Where is her nose compared with her eyes and chin? What do you notice about where her mouth and ears are placed?

Image **B** is a **self-portrait**. The artist painted a portrait of himself. Artists sometimes include things in self-portraits to tell about themselves. What can you tell about this artist from his self-portrait?

A Frida Kahlo,
Portrait of Virginia

B Henri Rousseau,
I Myself Portrait-Landscape

Artist's Workshop

Self-Portrait

PLAN . . . .

Think of some objects that tell something about you. Decide how you could include them in a self-portrait.

CREATE . . . .

1. Look at yourself in a mirror. Sketch your face on white paper.

2. Make sure you use proportion in your drawing. Use the diagram below to help you draw your eyes, nose, ears, and mouth.

3. Add details to your self-portrait with colored pencils. Include at least one object that tells something about you.

REFLECT . . . .

How did you use proportion in your self-portrait? What can people learn about you from your self-portrait?

Quick Tip

- The eyes are halfway between the top of the head and the bottom of the chin.

- The nose is halfway between the eyes and the chin, and the mouth is halfway between the nose and the chin.

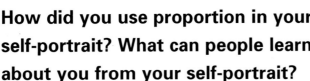

Family Scenes

A **seascape** is an artwork that shows a view of an ocean or a sea. Look at the seascape below. How would you describe this family scene? What do you think the people are doing?

Edward Potthast,
Play in the Surf

Artists create **movement** in an artwork to guide a viewer's eyes around the artwork. On the seascape on page 68, trace with your finger the path your eyes take around the artwork. What do you notice first? What do you notice next? Now trace the path to the part you notice last. One way artists create movement is by showing objects of different sizes. Did you notice small objects or large objects first?

Artist's Workshop

Family Scene Drawing

1. **Think about a time when your family worked together on something. Sketch your ideas.**

2. **Lightly trace a line to show how you want to guide viewers' eyes around the artwork. Draw the largest objects in the part of the artwork you want viewers to look at first.**

3. **Erase the guide line, and color your drawing.**

Henry Moore

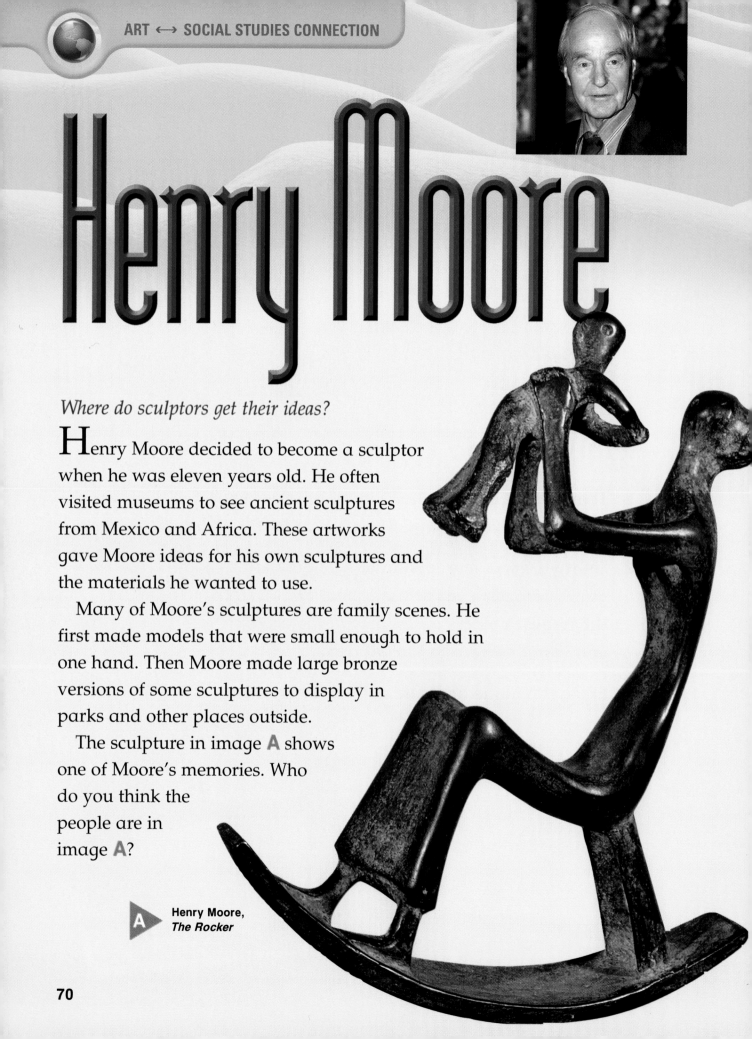

Where do sculptors get their ideas?

Henry Moore decided to become a sculptor when he was eleven years old. He often visited museums to see ancient sculptures from Mexico and Africa. These artworks gave Moore ideas for his own sculptures and the materials he wanted to use.

Many of Moore's sculptures are family scenes. He first made models that were small enough to hold in one hand. Then Moore made large bronze versions of some sculptures to display in parks and other places outside.

The sculpture in image **A** shows one of Moore's memories. Who do you think the people are in image **A**?

A Henry Moore, *The Rocker*

 B Henry Moore,
Study for a Family Group

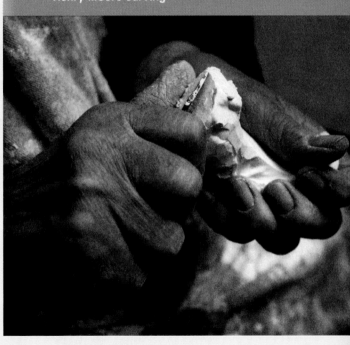

The sculpture in image **B** is a family scene. What family members do you see? How is image **B** different from image **A**? How are they alike?

Think About Art

What happy family memory might you show in a sculpture of your own? What materials would you use?

 **Multimedia Biographies**
Visit *The Learning Site*
www.harcourtschool.com

Patterns in Masks

People from many different cultures make masks. The mask in image **A** is from Africa. Describe the lines, shapes, and colors you see on the mask. Artists use repeating lines, shapes, and colors to create **patterns**. Point out a pattern of triangles in image **A**. Where on the mask do you see a pattern of curved lines?

The mask from Mexico in image **B** was made by gluing pieces of yarn to wood. Compare one side of the mask to the other side. The artist created **symmetry** by making one side of the mask match the other side. Does image **A** have symmetry? How can you tell?

A Unknown artist, African mask

B Unknown artist, Huichol yarn mask

Artist's Workshop

Mexican Yarn Mask

PLAN ....

Sketch some ideas for a mask that has symmetry. Repeat lines and shapes to make patterns.

CREATE ....

1. Draw your best idea on tagboard. Cut out the mask.

2. Outline the lines and shapes with glue. Press yarn onto the glue.

3. Glue a craft stick to the back to make a holder for your mask.

REFLECT ....

Describe the patterns on your mask. How did you show symmetry?

Quick Tip

Draw a straight line down the center of your mask. Match the patterns on each side of the line to show symmetry.

Patterns in Cloth

The image below shows a cloth panel called a **mola**. The Cuna people of Panama have been making molas for more than one hundred years. The colorful panels often show famous scenes. This mola shows a moon landing. What details do you see?

Artists make molas by sewing together layers of cloth. Each layer is a different color. Look at the edges of the spacecraft in the image below. What shape did the artist repeat to make a pattern? What other patterns do you see?

**Unknown artist,
Mola panel**

74

Artist's Workshop

Bird Mola

PLAN . . . .

Find a picture of a bird you like. Draw the shape of the bird in three different sizes. Cut out the shapes.

CREATE . . . .

1. Set aside one color of felt material for the bottom layer of your mola.

2. Use a marker to trace each shape onto a different color of felt material.

3. Cut out each shape from the center.

4. Glue the piece with the smallest cutout onto your bottom layer first. Glue down the piece with the medium cutout next and the piece with the largest cutout last.

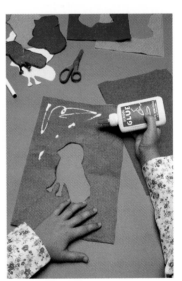

REFLECT . . . .

How did the layers of your mola make the design interesting?

Safety Tips As you cut, point the scissors away from your body.

Western Wear

How have cowboy boots changed over many years?

The first cowboys in the United States wore boots to make their jobs easier. The boots reached halfway up the cowboy's legs to protect him from snow, mud, and thorns. The toes of the boots were pointed so that cowboys could easily slip their feet into stirrups.

Zeferino and Eli Rios, Cowboy boots

Over time, cowboy boots have become popular with people who do not work on ranches or compete in rodeos. Artists have made special boots to show things that are important to the person who wears them. The boots in image **A** were a gift to President Dwight Eisenhower. The pictures on the boots tell about Washington, D.C., and Kansas, where President Eisenhower grew up.

Texas cowboy boot

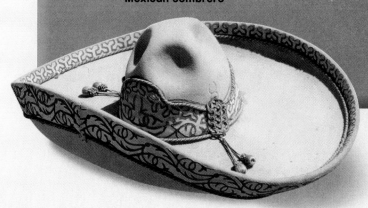

The design of the American cowboy hat was borrowed from Mexican sombreros like the one shown below. Sombreros were made with wide brims to protect Mexican cowboys, or vaqueros, from the hot sun.

Mexican sombrero

The boot in image **B** has the Texas flag on it. Why do you think someone might wear boots like this one?

The artist of image **C** used different kinds of lines to create a pattern. How would you describe this drawing to someone who has not seen it?

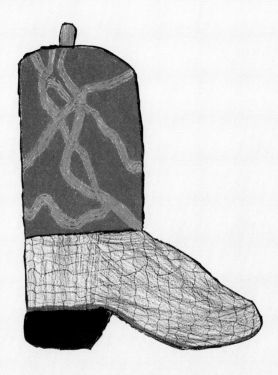

Think About Art

Imagine you are designing a pair of boots for yourself. What would you include to show what is important to you?

 Hannah, age 9, Cowboy boot drawing

77

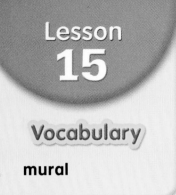

Mural Art

A **mural** is a large painting that covers a wall on the inside or the outside of a building. Image **A** shows a mural on a building in Mexico City, Mexico. Why do you think an artist would choose to paint murals instead of smaller paintings?

Murals often show people doing everyday things. Look at the crowded street in image **A**. How did the artist create movement in his mural? What path do your eyes take around it?

A Diego Rivera,
The Market

Image **B** is part of a large mural made by a group of children. What story do you think it tells about the United States? What kinds of patterns did the artists create in image **B**?

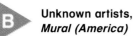 Unknown artists, *Mural (America)*

Artist's Workshop

Community Mural

1. **Work with a partner to brainstorm ideas for a mural about your community or another community. Then sketch one idea.**

2. **Transfer your sketch to a large sheet of butcher paper.**

3. **Think about how you want viewers' eyes to move around the mural. Place objects in the mural to create movement.**

4. **Paint your mural.**

Unit 3 Review and Reflect

Vocabulary and Concepts

Choose the letter of the word or phrase that best completes each sentence.

1 A ____ is an artwork that an artist paints of himself or herself.

   A portrait   **C** mural

   B self-portrait   **D** mola

2 ____ is the size and placement of some things compared with other things.

   A Movement   **C** Proportion

   B Pattern   **D** Symmetry

3 Artists create ____ to guide your eyes around an artwork.

   A portraits   **C** proportion

   B movement   **D** murals

4 Artists repeat lines, shapes, and colors to make ____.

   A patterns   **C** molas

   B proportion   **D** sculptures

5 A ____ is a large painting that covers a wall.

   A portrait   **C** seascape

   B mural   **D** mola

 **READING SKILL**

Narrative Elements

Look at the image on page 74. What story is the artist trying to tell? Use a story map like the one shown here to record your ideas.

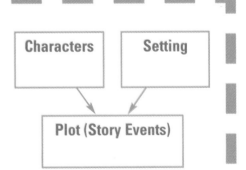

Write About Art

Write a story for one of your own artworks. Use a story map to plan your writing.

REMEMBER—YOU SHOULD

- describe the characters and setting of your story.

- tell the events in the plot.

- use correct grammar, spelling, and punctuation.

Critic's Corner

Look at the mural to answer the questions below.

Unknown artist,
Mural showing waterfront activities

DESCRIBE   What are the people in the artwork doing?

ANALYZE   How did the artist use proportion? What do you think the artist wanted viewers to see first?

INTERPRET   Do you think the artist wanted to create a calm feeling or a busy feeling? Why do you think so?

EVALUATE   Do you like the way this artwork shows people doing different activities? Why or why not?

Edward Hopper, *The Lighthouse at Two Lights*

LOCATE IT

This painting can be found at The Metropolitan Museum of Art in New York City.

See Maps of Museums and Art Sites, pages 144–147.

NEW YORK

New York City

Special Places

I'd Like to Be a Lighthouse

I'd like to be a lighthouse
   And scrubbed and painted white.
I'd like to be a lighthouse
   And stay awake all night
To keep my eye on everything
   That sails my patch of sea;
I'd like to be a lighthouse
   With the ships all watching me.

Rachel Field

Unit Vocabulary

horizon line	overlapping
space	center of interest
depth	emphasis
foreground	contrast
background	earthworks
cityscape	

ABOUT THE ARTIST

See Gallery of Artists, pages 178–188.

Multimedia Art Glossary
Visit *The Learning Site*
www.harcourtschool.com

Cause and Effect

A *cause* is the reason something happens. What happens is an *effect*.

Look at the images below. The artist painted the same subject at different times of the year.

- In image **A**, the cold weather and dim light caused the colors to look pale. The pale blues, grays, and white are effects of the cold and the dim light.

- In image **B**, the warm weather and bright sunlight caused the colors to be bright. The bright colors are effects of the bright sunlight.

 Claude Monet,
Landscape—Haystacks in the Snow

 Claude Monet,
Grainstacks in Bright Sunlight

You can also look for causes and effects to help you understand what you read. Find clues that tell what happened or why something happened. Read the passage below to find causes and effects.

> Claude Monet (moh•NAY) was a painter from France. He painted outdoors because he wanted to see how light and colors changed between different seasons and different times of the day. Beginning in 1890, Monet made more than thirty paintings of haystacks near his home. He also created many paintings of his own garden.

Why did Claude Monet paint outdoors? Use a diagram like this to write the cause and the effect.

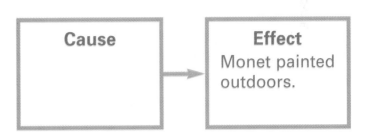

Cause

Effect
Monet painted outdoors.

On Your Own

As you read the lessons in this unit, use diagrams like the one above to write causes and effects that you find in the text and in the artworks.

Horizon Line

The place in an artwork where sky meets land or water is called the **horizon line**. In image **A**, the horizon line appears near the top of the painting. Find the horizon line in image **B**.

    Space is the area between and around objects. In two-dimensional artworks, artists create the feeling of space, or **depth**, by making some objects seem to be closer to the viewer than others. An object that is placed farther below the horizon line seems to be closer to the viewer. Look at image **A**. Which boat seems to be closer to the viewer?

Arturo Gordon,
*Boats Together
at the Sea*

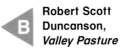
Robert Scott Duncanson, *Valley Pasture*

Point out the large rocks and the water in image B.
Do the rocks or the water seem to be closer to you?
How can you tell?

Artist's Workshop

Saltwater Seascape

1. **Draw your seascape on watercolor paper. Think about how much sky you want to show in your painting.**

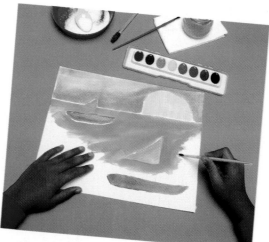

2. **To create depth, draw an object near the horizon line and another object far below it.**

3. **Paint your seascape with watercolors.**

4. **Before the paint dries, create texture by sprinkling salt on the part of your painting that shows water.**

Depth in Landscapes

When you look out your window, do faraway objects seem smaller or larger than nearby objects? Artists can create the feeling of depth by changing the size of objects in their artworks.

Look at the image below. The area at the bottom of the artwork is the **foreground**. The foreground is the part of the artwork that seems closest to the viewer. What do you see in the foreground of this image?

Now look at the area near the horizon line. This is the **background**. The background is the part of the artwork that seems farthest away. What objects do you see in the background? Does the horse in the foreground seem smaller or larger than the horse in the background?

Ando Hiroshige,
Fuji from Kogane-Ga-Hara, Shimosa

Artist's Workshop

Landscape Drawing

PLAN ....

Look at pictures of outdoor scenes to sketch ideas for a landscape.

CREATE ....

1. **Fold a sheet of paper into three equal sections. Then open it up.**

2. **Draw a line in pencil along the highest fold. This will be your horizon line.**

3. **The lowest section of your paper is the foreground. Draw the largest objects in the foreground.**

4. **The middle section of your paper is the background. Draw the smallest objects in the background.**

5. **Use colored pencils to add details.**

REFLECT ....

Look at your completed landscape. How did you create depth?

You can also add depth to your drawing by using light values in the background and dark values in the foreground.

Forces in Nature

How was the Grand Canyon formed?

The Grand Canyon in Arizona is a popular subject of artworks. The Colorado River, shown in image **A**, cut into layers of rock to form the deep canyon.

Few people knew about the Grand Canyon until 1869. At that time, an explorer named John Wesley Powell traveled by boat along the Colorado River and saw how the river had cut through the land.

 A The Colorado River in the Grand Canyon

B Carl Oscar Borg, *Grand Canyon*

Powell took artists to the Grand Canyon to paint pictures for many people to see. Artists are still painting the canyon. In image **B**, what part of the canyon seems closest to the viewer? What part seems farthest away?

Think About Art

Would you rather paint the Grand Canyon from the bottom of the canyon looking up or from the top looking down? How would these views be different?

Overlapping Lines and Shapes

A **cityscape** is an artwork that shows a city view. Look at the cityscapes in images **A** and **B**. What time of day does each one show?

Now look at the buildings in image **A**. Find one building that overlaps, or partly covers, part of another building. Artists can use **overlapping** to show that one object is closer to the viewer than another object. Which buildings in image **A** seem closest to the viewer? Find lines, such as the tall streetlights, that also cover parts of the artwork.

A **Red Grooms,**
Looking Along
Broadway Towards
Grace Church

The artist of image **B** also used overlapping. Which objects in image **B** seem closest to the viewer? Why?

B Laura, grade 3, *City Lights*

Artist's Workshop

Cityscape Painting

1. **Look at pictures of buildings and cities to get ideas for your cityscape. Sketch one idea.**

2. **Draw your cityscape on construction paper. Use overlapping to show the buildings that are closest to the viewer.**

3. **Paint your cityscape. Then add details with markers.**

Center of Interest

Look at the painting below. What do you notice first? Why do you think this is so?

The part of an artwork that an artist wants you to see first is called the **center of interest**. Artists use **emphasis** to make the viewer look at the center of interest. One way to create emphasis in an artwork is to use contrast. Lines, shapes, textures, and colors that are very different from each other have **contrast**.

Look at how the artist used contrasting colors to create emphasis in the painting below. The bright colors on the toy car make it stand out. How are these colors different from the colors in the background?

Reynard Milici, *The Cozy Coupe*

Artist's Workshop

Outdoor Scene

PLAN

Sketch an idea for an outdoor scene. Choose one object in the scene to be your center of interest.

CREATE

1. Copy your sketch onto white paper.

2. Think about your center of interest. Create emphasis by using contrasting lines, shapes, textures, or colors.

3. Add details to your drawing with colored pencils.

REFLECT

Look at your finished drawing. How did you show emphasis?

Quick Tip

You can show emphasis by using contrasting shapes. For example, you can make a geometric shape stand out by placing it in a scene with many organic shapes.

Winslow Homer

What were Winslow Homer's favorite subjects to paint?

As a child, Winslow Homer enjoyed playing outdoors in the Massachusetts countryside. His mother was a painter, and Homer was interested in art from an early age.

Homer became known for his paintings of children and nature. In many of Homer's paintings, you can see his childhood memories. Look at image A. What might the children in this painting be thinking about?

 A **Winslow Homer, *Boys in a Pasture***

B Winslow Homer, *The Boat Builders*

The children in image B are building toy boats. Look at the background of the painting. Why do you think Homer showed a toy boat overlapping a real sailboat? What do you notice when you compare the sizes of the toy boat and the real sailboat?

DID YOU KNOW?

Children in nearly every culture play with the same kinds of toys. Even children in ancient times had toys such as dolls, balls, and toy animals. Most toys are small copies of larger objects. Why do you think the same kinds of toys have been popular with children for many years?

Think About Art

Why do you think Winslow Homer made many paintings of the same subject? What subject would you like to paint in different ways?

GO ONLINE **Multimedia Biographies**
Visit *The Learning Site*
www.harcourtschool.com

Art in Nature

Earthworks are artworks that are designed to be outdoors and are made of natural materials. Artists who make earthworks arrange their materials in natural environments. They can create emphasis by using contrasting lines, shapes, colors, forms, or textures.

Look at the garden in image . How did the artist create emphasis? What kinds of lines, shapes, and forms did the artist who designed this garden use?

A Ornamental Municipal Gardens in Angers, France

98

Now look at image **B**. The artists surrounded real islands with floating fabric. Why do you think the artists used the color pink? Would you notice this artwork from a distance if the artist had used blue fabric instead?

 B Christo and Jeanne-Claude,
Surrounded Islands

Artist's Workshop

Garden Design

1. **Think of a garden design you would like to create. Picture what the garden would look like from above.**

2. **Draw your garden design on white paper. Draw different shapes to show how the plants would be arranged.**

3. **Include a path for people to walk on in your garden.**

4. **Use crayons or colored pencils to color your garden design.**

Unit 4 Review and Reflect

Vocabulary and Concepts

Choose the letter of the word or phrase that best completes each sentence.

1 ___ is the area between and around objects.

   A Space   **C** Depth

   B Emphasis   **D** Symmetry

2 The ___ is the place in an artwork where the sky meets the land.

   A foreground   **C** background

   B emphasis   **D** horizon line

3 Artists place smaller objects in the background of a painting to show ___.

   A overlapping   **C** emphasis

   B depth   **D** pattern

4 Artists use ___ to show that one object is in front of another object.

   A proportion   **C** contrast

   B overlapping   **D** movement

5 Artworks that are set outdoors and made of natural materials are ___.

   A cityscapes   **C** seascapes

   B earthworks   **D** murals

 **READING SKILL**

Cause and Effect

Reread the information on page 90. Then use a cause-and-effect diagram to tell how the Grand Canyon was formed.

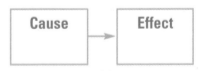

Write About Art

Write a story about the artwork on page 92. Tell what caused the street to become so busy. Then tell the effect of the busy street on people who live in the city. Use a diagram to plan your writing.

REMEMBER—YOU SHOULD

- explain at least one cause and one effect.

- use correct grammar, spelling, and punctuation.

Critic's Corner

Look at *Boats on the Beach* by Vincent van Gogh to answer the questions below.

DESCRIBE   What is the subject of this painting?

ANALYZE   How did the artist show depth? How did he create emphasis?

INTERPRET   Why do you think the artist wanted to show this place?

EVALUATE   Does the painting show a place you would like to visit? Why or why not?

Vincent van Gogh, *Boats on the Beach*

Paul Klee, *Seascape*

LOCATE IT

The Paul Klee Centre is located in Berne, Switzerland.
It contains more than 10,000 artworks by Paul Klee.

See Maps of Museum and Art Sites, pages 144–147.

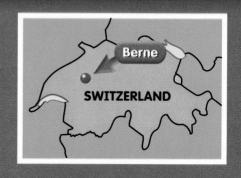

Berne

SWITZERLAND

5

Surprising Viewpoints

Waves of the Sea

Waves of the sea
make the sound of thunder
when they break against rocks
and somersault under.

Waves of the sea
make the sound of laughter
when they run down the beach
and birds run after.

Aileen Fisher

Unit Vocabulary

grid	distortion
symmetrical	unity
balance	complementary colors
asymmetrical	neutral colors
balance	collage
abstract art	

ABOUT THE ARTIST

See Gallery of Artists,
pages 178–188.

Multimedia Art Glossary
Visit *The Learning Site*
www.harcourtschool.com

Fact and Opinion

A *fact* is something that can be proved. An *opinion* is a person's own belief or feeling.

You can discuss artworks by sharing facts and your own opinions. Look at the artwork in the image below. Then read the facts and opinion about it.

- **Facts** The artwork is a sculpture. The artist painted it black, red, and blue.

- **Opinion** The artwork is one of the finest in the world.

Do you agree with the opinion? What are some other facts about the artwork?

Alexander Calder, *Myxomatose*

You can look for facts and opinions to help you understand what you read. Read the passage below. Look for facts and opinions about the artist.

A mobile is a sculpture that has moving parts. Alexander Calder was one of the first artists to become known for making mobiles. In some of his mobiles, parts are moved by a small motor. In others, parts are moved by the wind or by air blowing on them. Many other artists have created wonderful mobiles. However, Calder's are the best.

What information in the passage can be proved? What opinions did the author include? Use a chart like this one to write facts and opinions.

Facts	Opinions
A small motor moves parts in some of Calder's mobiles.	

On Your Own

As you read the lessons in this unit, use charts like the one above to write facts and opinions about the text and the artworks.

Symmetrical Balance

Look closely at image **A**. What is unusual about this painting? The artist created image **A** on a **grid**, a pattern of squares of equal size. She placed dots of color in each space on the grid. What shapes do the dots make?

Trace your finger down the middle of image **A**. What do you notice about the two sides? Artists can create **symmetrical balance** by using lines, shapes, and colors to make one side of an artwork match the other side.

grid

A   **Jennifer Bartlett,**
Red House Painting

Artists can also create symmetrical balance by placing similar objects on opposite sides of the artwork. What does the painting in image **B** show? Choose one object in the painting. Then look for a similar object on the other side of the painting. Does symmetrical balance create a tidy feeling or messy feeling in this painting?

 Patssi Valdez, *Fenye's House Dining Room*

Artist's Workshop

Grid Drawing

1. **Think of an object or scene that has symmetrical balance. Sketch some ideas.**

2. **Draw a line down the middle of a sheet of graph paper.**

3. **Lightly draw your picture. Count the number of boxes in each shape to make sure you have symmetrical balance.**

4. **Color in the boxes. Use the same colors for matching shapes on each side of the middle line.**

Asymmetrical Balance

When the two sides of an artwork do not match each other, the artwork can still be balanced. Artists can use different lines, shapes, and colors to give the artwork **asymmetrical balance**.

Look at the painting below. Notice that the window frame is not in the middle of the painting. The tall tree on the right is balanced by the column of squares on the left. How are the shapes of these objects different?

Now look at the colors the artist used. What part of the painting shows mostly warm colors? Where do you see mostly cool colors?

Pablo Picasso, *The Pigeons*

Artist's Workshop

Window View Drawing

PLAN

Imagine how a city at night might look from the window of a tall building. Sketch your ideas.

CREATE

1. Draw a window frame on the left or right side of your paper. Then draw a city scene inside the window frame.

2. Draw some objects inside the room. Use different shapes to create asymmetrical balance.

3. Add color to your drawing with oil pastels. Blend the colors with a cotton swab.

REFLECT

What shapes and colors did you use to create asymmetrical balance?

Quick Tip

You may want to use geometric shapes to show tall buildings outside the window. Balance these shapes by using organic shapes for objects inside the room.

Patricia Polacco: Storyteller

A **Patricia Polacco, Book cover for *Appelemando's Dreams* LITERATURE LINK**

Where do storytellers get their ideas?

Storytelling was an important part of Patricia Polacco's childhood. Both of her parents passed down stories to her from their different cultures. When Polacco was young, she loved to tell stories. Later, she began writing them down.

Now Polacco writes and illustrates children's books. She often uses memories from her own life as story ideas. Once she has finished writing a story, Polacco creates an illustration for each page of the book.

The illustration on page 111 is from Polacco's book called *Appelemando's Dreams*. In this story, a boy uses his imagination to create colorful dreams that his whole town can see. How did Polacco show Appelemando's imagination in image **B**?

Artists and writers often work for months or even years on a book. Once Patricia Polacco gets an idea for a book, a year and a half might go by before you can buy that book in a bookstore. Polacco spends about five months writing and illustrating a story. Another year or more is needed to make the stories and pictures into a book.

B Patricia Polacco, Illustration from *Appelemando's Dreams*

Think About Art

What life experiences would you include in a story about yourself? What would the illustrations look like?

Abstract Portraits

An artwork that shows something exactly as it looks in real life is realistic art. **Abstract art** is not realistic. The painting in image **A** is an abstract portrait. Find the subject's eyes, nose, mouth, and hands. What shapes and colors did the artist use to paint these features? Does the painting have symmetrical or asymmetrical balance?

Distortion can be seen in many abstract artworks. When artists use **distortion**, they change the way an object looks by bending or stretching its shape. Look at the abstract portrait in image **B**. Where has the artist used distortion?

A Juan Gris, *Clown*

B Taylor, grade 3, Untitled

Artist's Workshop

Abstract Self-Portrait

PLAN

Sketch a self-portrait. Think about how you can add distortion by changing the shapes of your facial features.

CREATE

1. **Copy your sketch onto white paper.**

2. **Use geometric shapes for the parts of your face. Erase parts of your sketch, and change or break up the shapes to create distortion.**

3. **Add different kinds of lines to the background to show your feelings.**

4. **Paint your self-portrait.**

REFLECT

What shapes did you use in your painting? How did you show distortion?

Quick Tip

Mix tints and shades of your favorite color to show your personality in your painting.

Abstract Designs

The painting below has an abstract design. It does not show any objects from real life. Look at the repeated lines, shapes, and colors. When the parts of an artwork seem to belong together, the artist has created a feeling of **unity**. Would this painting look complete if some of the shapes were missing? Why or why not?

Now find places in the painting where the colors red and green are next to each other. Red and green are complementary colors. **Complementary colors** are opposite each other on the color wheel. When complementary colors are placed side by side in an artwork, they create a lively feeling. What other complementary colors do you see in this painting?

Artists can create **neutral colors**, such as brown and gray, by mixing complementary colors. Where do you see neutral colors in this painting?

Sonia Delaunay, *Composition*

Artist's Workshop

Abstract Painting

PLAN

Sketch repeated lines and shapes to create an abstract design. Then choose a pair of complementary colors to use in your painting.

CREATE

1. Copy your sketch onto white paper. You may need to add lines and shapes to create a feeling of unity.

2. Mix small amounts of your complementary colors to create neutral colors.

3. Paint your design. Use only the two complementary colors and the neutral colors you have mixed.

REFLECT

What complementary colors and neutral colors did you use? How did you show unity in your painting?

Quick Tip

You can make tints and shades of neutral colors by mixing them with black and white.

ROMARE BEARDEN

 Romare Bearden,
Gospel Song

What inspired many of Romare Bearden's artworks?

Romare Bearden grew up listening to the sounds of jazz music. Bearden's father had many friends who were musicians, and they gathered at the Bearden home to play music together. Bearden also heard the musicians who played on the street corners near his home in Harlem, New York.

Romare Bearden,
The Piano Lesson
(Homage to Mary Lou)

Bearden's interest in music can be seen in many of his artworks. He often created artworks that have musicians and instruments as subjects. Look at image **A**. What is the subject of this artwork? Does image **A** make you think of a slow song or a song with a fast rhythm? Why? What kind of music does image **B** remind you of?

DID YOU KNOW?

In the 1920s, many African Americans used art to express feelings about their culture. This period was called the Harlem Renaissance because most of these artists worked in Harlem, New York. Writers, musicians, and artists were part of the Harlem Renaissance. Romare Bearden was one of these artists.

THINK ABOUT ART

Think about the music you like best. What kinds of lines, shapes, and colors could you use to show it in an artwork?

GO
ONLINE

Multimedia Biographies
Visit *The Learning Site*
www.harcourtschool.com

Collage

A **collage** is an artwork made by gluing pieces of paper and other material to a flat surface. A collage artist may use cut paper, photographs, fabric, or other kinds of scraps.

The artist of image A made collages of indoor scenes. He often cut pictures from popular advertisements. Look at the different objects in image A. Why does everything seem to belong in this scene? How did this artist create a feeling of unity?

A Tom Wesselmann, *Still Life #25*

Now look at image **B**. This abstract collage is made of wood, fabric, metal, and paper. Why do you think the artist of image **B** used different textures in his collage? How is the collage in image **B** different from the collage in image **A**?

 B
Kurt Schwitters,
Merz Picture 32A. (The Cherry Picture)

Artist's Workshop

Multi-Texture Collage

1. **Find a picture of an interesting scene in a magazine or book. Think about materials and textures you can use to show the scene as a collage.**

2. **Draw the shapes for your collage on the materials you have chosen. Use repeated colors, shapes, and textures to create unity. Cut out the shapes.**

3. **Arrange the shapes on a background. Then glue down the shapes.**

Unit 5 Review and Reflect

Vocabulary and Concepts

Choose the letter of the word or phrase that best completes each sentence.

1 Artworks that match on two sides have ___.

  A asymmetrical balance   **C** symmetrical balance

  B unity   **D** distortion

2 ___ colors are opposite each other on the color wheel.

  A Complementary   **C** Primary

  B Secondary   **D** Neutral

3 A ___ is made by gluing different materials to a flat surface.

  A mural   **C** collage

  B weaving   **D** cityscape

4 Artworks that do not match on both sides have ___.

  A emphasis   **C** depth

  B asymmetrical balance   **D** symmetrical balance

5 When the parts of an artwork seem to belong together, the artwork has ___.

  A movement   **C** distortion

  B unity   **D** balance

Focus Skill READING SKILL

Fact and Opinion

Reread the information about Romare Bearden on pages 116–117. Write facts from the text in a chart like the one shown here. Then write your opinions about Romare Bearden and his artworks.

Facts	Opinions

Write About Art

Write a paragraph about one of the artworks in this unit.
Include facts and your own opinions about the artwork.
Use a chart to plan your writing.

REMEMBER—YOU SHOULD

- write information that can be proved.

- write your opinions about the artwork.

- use correct grammar, spelling, and punctuation.

Critic's Corner

Look at *Morning in the Village after Snowstorm* by Kasimir
Malevich to answer the questions below.

DESCRIBE   What is the subject of the painting?

ANALYZE   Is the painting abstract or realistic? Where did the artist use complementary colors? How did the artist create unity?

INTERPRET   What do you think the artist was trying to say about the village in the painting?

EVALUATE   Do you think the artist got his message across? Why or why not?

Kasimir Malevich, *Morning in the Village after Snowstorm*

Unknown artist, *Chariot of the Sun*

LOCATE IT

This artwork can be found at the National Museum of Denmark.

See Maps of Museum and Art Sites, pages 144–147.

DENMARK

Copenhagen

Old and New Ideas

The Sun

I told the Sun that I was glad,
    I'm sure I don't know why;
Somehow the pleasant way he had
    Of shining in the sky,
Just put a notion in my head
    That wouldn't it be fun
If, walking on the hill, I said
    "I'm happy" to the Sun.

John Drinkwater

Unit Vocabulary

symbol	photomontage
variety	assemblage
prints	found objects
rhythm	graphic arts

Multimedia Art Glossary
Visit *The Learning Site*
www.harcourtschool.com

123

Summarize

When you *summarize*, you tell the most important ideas in one or two sentences.

Look at the scenes in the painting below. You can summarize what is happening in the painting by looking for the most important ideas.

- **Important Idea** Each scene shows children playing a different game.

- **Important Idea** The children are playing outdoors.

- **Summary** Children are playing different games outdoors.

Anna Belle Lee Washington, *Games We Played*

You can also summarize information in text to help you understand what you read. When you summarize text, you retell the most important ideas in your own words. Read the passage below, looking for the most important ideas.

When Anna Belle Lee Washington was a child, she never thought she would become a well-known artist. As an adult, Washington began painting as a hobby. Her paintings first became popular with her neighbors in St. Simons Island, Georgia. Now Washington's paintings can be seen on book covers and in museums around the world.

What are the important ideas in this passage? How can you combine them into a summary? Use a diagram like this to help you.

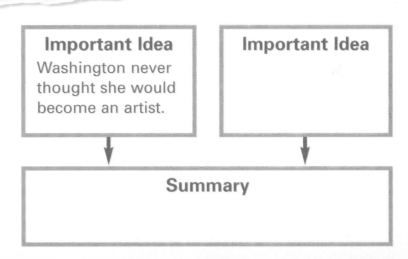

Important Idea
Washington never thought she would become an artist.

Important Idea

Summary

On Your Own

As you read the lessons in this unit, use diagrams like the one above to summarize the text and the ideas in the artworks.

Shapes and Symbols

A **symbol** is a shape that stands for an idea. In ancient times, people used symbols instead of words to send messages to one another. Look at the symbols on the ancient artwork in image **A**. What do you think they might stand for? Artists today may also use symbols in their artworks. The painted sun on the jug in image **B** might be a symbol for warmth or light.

Artists create **variety** in artworks by using contrasting lines, shapes, and colors. Variety can make an artwork more interesting. What contrasting colors and lines did the artist of image **B** use to show variety?

A Unknown artist, Egyptian hieroglyphics

B Clarice Cliff,
'Sun Ray' Double-Handled Lotus Jug

Artist's Workshop

Clay Pinch Pot

PLAN ·

Think of some symbols that tell about you or about something that is important to you. Sketch these symbols.

CREATE ·

1. Make a clay ball about the size of an orange.

2. Press your thumbs into the ball to make a dent. Keep pressing your thumbs out from the center to make the sides of your pot. Pinch the sides of your pot evenly all the way around.

3. Carve symbols and lines onto the sides of your pot. Use different symbols and lines to create variety.

REFLECT ·

What do the symbols on your pinch pot stand for? How did you create variety?

As you carve, press lightly so that you do not make a hole through your pot.

Printmaking

Images **A** and **B** show examples of prints. To make **prints**, artists paint a design on a flat object or printing block. While the paint is still wet, they press the block onto a piece of paper. Artists can create many prints by using the same printing block.

Look at the print in image **A**. What shapes are repeated? Artists can create **rhythm** in an artwork by repeating lines, shapes, colors, or patterns. Rhythm guides your eyes around the artwork. It can also make you feel a certain way. Does the print in image **A** remind you of a summer day or a winter day? Why?

A Beatricia Sagar, *Sun Shines*

Tanaya, grade 4, Untitled

The artist of image **B** created rhythm by printing the same design four times. How do your eyes move around image **B**? How did the artist create variety?

Artist's Workshop

Kaleidoscope Print

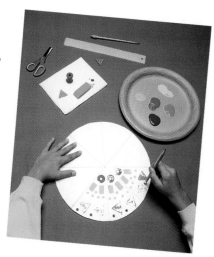

1. **Use a large paper plate to trace the shape of a circle onto white paper. Use a ruler and a pencil to divide your circle into eight pie-shaped pieces. Cut out the circle.**

2. **Pour small amounts of different paint colors onto your plate. Dip different small objects into the paint. Press them onto a section of your cutout circle.**

3. **Repeat the same design in each section of your circle to create rhythm.**

Styles of Architecture

What do architects do?

Architects are people who design schools, houses, airports, hospitals, and other buildings. The museums in images **A** and **B** were also designed by architects.

The museum in image **A** was built in 1917. It is located in an old Spanish plaza in Santa Fe, New Mexico, one of the oldest cities in North America. The museum was designed in the Spanish-Pueblo style. In this style, buildings are made of adobe, a mixture of clay, mud, and straw. Many of the buildings in the Santa Fe plaza are made in the Spanish-Pueblo style in order to keep alive the history and traditions of the city.

 A John Gaw Meem, Santa Fe Museum of Fine Arts

The building in image **B** was built in Bilbao, Spain, in 1997. The architect designed the glass walls to protect the artworks inside from heat. How would you describe this building?

Architects make drawings and build models of their designs. Models show what a building will look like when it is finished. The model below was created for a house in California.

Frank O. Gehry, Architect's model

 Frank O. Gehry, Guggenheim Bilbao

Think About Art

Describe the style of the buildings in your community. What do you think they are made of?

Rhythm in Photomontage

Louise Freshman-Brown,
Interior with Red Apples

The image above is a photomontage. A **photomontage** is made by cutting out parts of different photographs and arranging them in an interesting way. Look carefully at the artwork above. What kinds of objects do you see?

The artist of this photomontage used photographs with many different patterns. The repeating lines, colors, and shapes in the patterns give the artwork rhythm. How do your eyes move around the artwork? Do the contrasting patterns in this artwork give you a peaceful feeling or a restless feeling?

Artist's Workshop

Photomontage

PLAN ·

Think about a scene or idea you want to show in a photomontage. Look for magazine pictures to use in your artwork.

CREATE ·

1. Cut out pictures with similar shapes, colors, or patterns.

2. Arrange your pictures on a sheet of construction paper.

3. Create rhythm by using pictures with similar shapes, colors, or patterns.

4. Glue your pictures to the construction paper.

REFLECT ·

Look at your finished photomontage. How did you create rhythm?

Quick Tip

Create depth in your photomontage by overlapping pictures. Use larger pictures in the background.

Assemblage

An **assemblage** is a sculpture made of different objects and materials. Artists who make assemblages often use **found objects**, or everyday objects they find, in their artworks. Look at the assemblage shown in image **A**. What found objects did the artist use in his artwork? What lines, shapes, colors, and forms did he use to create variety?

Image **B** shows an assemblage made of found pieces of wood. What forms did this artist include in her artwork? What textures did she use?

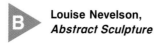

A David Stewart,
World Series

B Louise Nevelson,
Abstract Sculpture

134

Artist's Workshop

Found-Object Assemblage

PLAN ....

Gather some found objects to use in your assemblage. Practice arranging them in different ways.

CREATE ....

1. Paint the objects in your assemblage. Use different colors to create variety.

2. Arrange your objects inside a shoe box. Make sure to put objects in each corner of your box.

3. Glue your objects into place.

REFLECT ....

Look at your finished assemblage. What found objects did you use? How did you create variety?

Quick Tip

Glue smaller objects onto larger objects to add interest to your assemblage.

Nicario Jimenez

 Nicario Jimenez, *Art Festival*

What are retablos?

Nicario Jimenez is an artist from Peru known for making retablos. A retablo is a wooden box filled with figures that show a scene from daily life. What scene does the retablo in image **A** show?

The tiny figures that Jimenez creates are made from a mixture of boiled potatoes and a special powder. To carve details, he uses a small wooden tool that looks like a toothpick. Then he paints the figures. The boxes themselves are also painted as part of the artwork.

The retablo in image **B** shows a weaver's workshop. Notice the tiny workers and the finished weavings. What other details do you see in this retablo?

Think About Art

What scene would you show in your own retablo?

B Nicario Jimenez,
Weaver's Workshop

Graphic Arts

Most paintings and sculptures must be viewed in museums or art galleries. **Graphic arts**, such as advertisements, can be viewed almost anywhere. Artists create images that can be printed over and over in magazines, on posters and billboards, and on television.

Image **A** is an advertisement for oranges. The artist has included details to help people remember the product. What would you remember about this advertisement? How did the artist create variety?

 Cactus Brand Oranges—Highland Fruit Growers Association, Promotional literature posters

Now look at image **B**. What does this poster advertise? This graphic artist used a computer drawing program to draw and color her artwork. What lines, shapes, and colors did she use to create variety?

WE'RE WAITING JUST FOR
YOU AT THE ZOO

Johanna Kriesel,
"We're Waiting Just for You at the Zoo" Panda Print

Artist's Workshop

Graphic Design

1. **Design the front of a cereal box. Think of a name for your cereal, and sketch some ideas.**

2. **Use colored pencils and paper to create your design. Include letters and details to help people remember your product.**

3. **Use different lines, shapes, and colors to create variety.**

139

Unit 6 Review and Reflect

Vocabulary and Concepts

Choose the letter of the word or phrase that best completes each sentence.

1 A ___ is a shape that stands for an idea.

    A print   **C** symbol

    B found object   **D** pattern

2 Artists can use contrasting lines, shapes, and colors to create ___.

    A variety   **C** rhythm

    B movement   **D** unity

3 Artists can create ___ by repeating lines, shapes, colors, and patterns.

    A variety   **C** emphasis

    B rhythm   **D** distortion

4 Artists use cut photographs to create ___.

    A graphic arts   **C** murals

    B photomontages **D** prints

5 ___ are sculptures made of found objects and other materials.

    A Assemblages   **C** Prints

    B Weavings   **D** Symbols

READING SKILL

Summarize

Reread the first paragraph on page 128. Look for the most important ideas. Then summarize the paragraph. Use a diagram like the one shown here to help you.

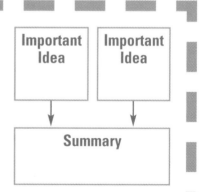

Write About Art

Reread the information about Nicario Jimenez on page 136. Then write a summary of the text. Use a diagram to organize your ideas.

REMEMBER—YOU SHOULD

- tell the most important ideas in your own words.

- use correct grammar, spelling, and punctuation.

Critic's Corner

Look at *Mercedes-Benz Type C111 prototype* by Andy Warhol to answer the questions below.

DESCRIBE What is the subject of the painting?

ANALYZE How did the artist create rhythm in his painting? How did he create variety?

INTERPRET Does the painting seem old, or does it seem modern? Why do you think so?

EVALUATE Is this a painting you will remember? Why or why not?

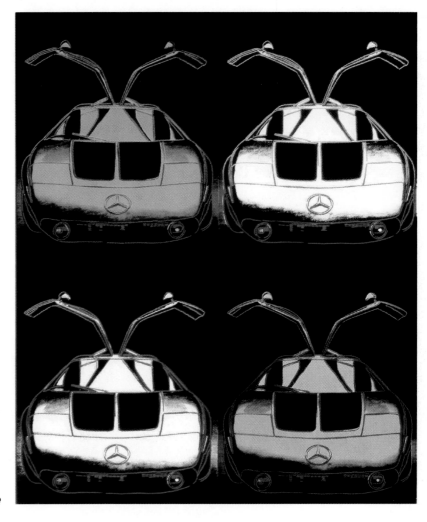

Andy Warhol,
Mercedes-Benz Type C111 prototype

Student Handbook

C O N T E N T S

15 Museums and Art Sites
United States

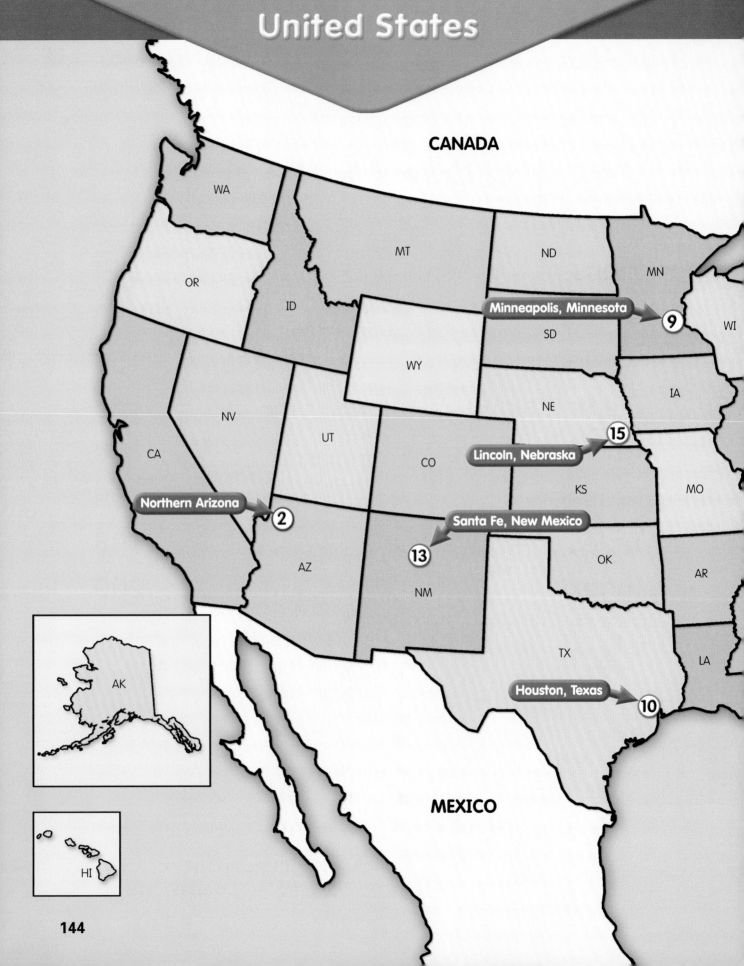

CANADA

WA

OR

ID

MT

ND

MN

WI

SD

Minneapolis, Minnesota ➤ (9)

WY

IA

NV

UT

CO

NE

Lincoln, Nebraska ➤ (15)

CA

MO

KS

Northern Arizona ➤ (2)

AZ

NM

Santa Fe, New Mexico
(13) ◄

OK

AR

AK

TX

LA

Houston, Texas ➤ (10)

HI

MEXICO

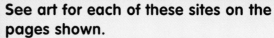

LOCATE IT

See art for each of these sites on the pages shown.

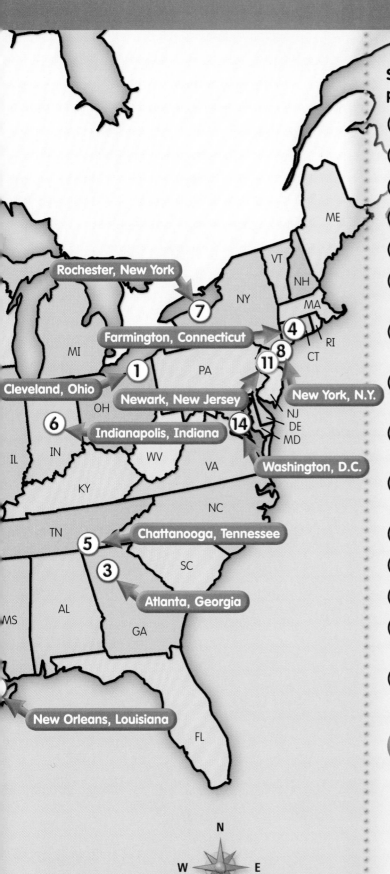

Rochester, New York
Farmington, Connecticut
Cleveland, Ohio
Newark, New Jersey
New York, N.Y.
Indianapolis, Indiana
Washington, D.C.
Chattanooga, Tennessee
Atlanta, Georgia
New Orleans, Louisiana

ME
VT
NH
NY
MA
RI
CT
MI
PA
OH
NJ
DE
MD
IN
IL
WV
VA
KY
NC
TN
SC
AL
GA
MS
FL

N
W E
S

① **The Cleveland Museum of Art,** page 92

② **Grand Canyon National Park,** page 90

③ **High Museum of Art,** page 14

④ **Hill-Stead Museum,** page 84

⑤ **Hunter Museum,** page 44

⑥ **The Indianapolis Museum of Art,** page 97

⑦ **Memorial Art Gallery of the University of Rochester,** page 116

⑧ **The Metropolitan Museum of Art,** page 82

⑨ **The Minneapolis Institute of Arts,** page 126

⑩ **The Museum of Fine Arts, Houston,** page 14

⑪ **The Newark Museum,** page 88

⑫ **New Orleans Museum of Art,** page 48

⑬ **Santa Fe Museum of Fine Arts,** page 130

⑭ **Smithsonian American Art Museum,** pages 28, 35, 50, 51, and 91

⑮ **University of Nebraska-Lincoln,** page 42

 Use the Electronic Art Gallery CD-ROM, Primary, to locate artworks from other museums and art sites.

15 Museums and Art Sites
World

St. Petersburg, Russia

Copenhagen, Denmark

5

Berlin, Germany

NORTH AMERICA

EUROPE

13

11

12 **14**

Berne, Switzerland

15

Washington, D.C.

Paris, France

Nayarit, Mexico

Heracleopolis, Egypt

4

8 **10**

AFRICA

Mexico City, Mexico

7

San Blas, Panama

2

Colombia

3

SOUTH AMERICA

Peru

6

Valparaiso, Chile

N

W E

S

ANTARCTICA

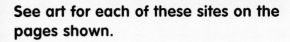

LOCATE IT

See art for each of these sites on the pages shown.

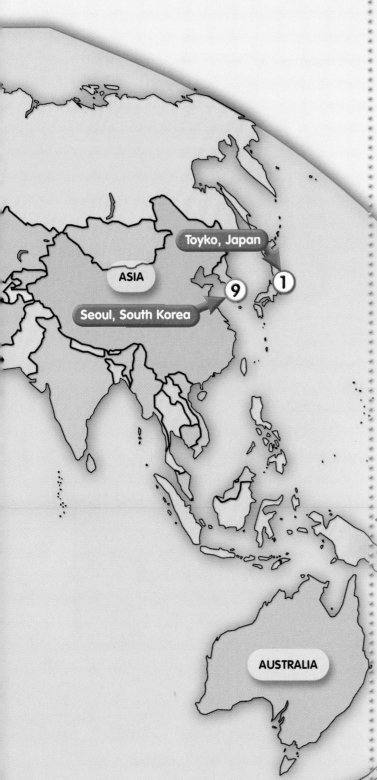

Art Safety

Listen carefully when your teacher explains how to use art materials.

Read the labels on materials before you use them.

Tell your teacher if you have allergies.

Wear a smock or apron to keep your clothes clean.

Use tools carefully. Hold sharp objects so that they cannot hurt you or others. Wear safety glasses to protect your eyes.

Use the kind of markers and inks that will not stain your clothes.

Clean up spills right away so no one will slip and fall.

Always wash your hands after using art materials.

Show respect for other students. Walk carefully around their work. Never touch classmates' work without asking first.

Cover your skin if you have a cut or scratch.

Art Techniques

Trying Ways to Draw

There are lots of ways to draw. You can sketch quickly to show a rough idea of your subject, or you can draw carefully to show just how it looks to you. Try to draw every day. Keep your drawings in your sketchbook so you can see how your drawing skills improve.

Here are some ideas for drawing. To start, get out some pencils and either your sketchbook or a sheet of paper.

GESTURE DRAWING

Gesture drawings are quick sketches that are made with loose arm movements. The gesture drawing on the left shows a rough idea of what a baseball player looks like. The more careful drawing on the right shows details of the player's uniform and face. ▶

◀ **Find some photographs of people or animals.** Make gesture drawings of them. Draw quickly. Don't try to show details.

◀ **Ask a friend to pose for a gesture drawing.** Take no more than two or three minutes to finish your sketch.

CONTOUR DRAWING

Contour drawings show only the outlines of the shapes that make up objects. They do not show the objects' color or shading. The lines that go around shapes are called **contour lines.** Use your finger to trace around the contour lines of the truck in this picture. Trace the lines around each of the shapes that make up the truck.

A blind contour drawing is made without looking at your paper as you draw. Choose a simple object to draw, like a leaf. Pick a point on the object where you will begin drawing. Move your eyes slowly around the edge of the object. Without looking at your paper, move your pencil in the same way that your eyes move. Your first drawings may not look like the object you are looking at. Practice with different objects to improve your skill.

Continuous contour drawings are made without lifting your pencil off the paper. Draw something simple, like a chair. Look back and forth between the object and your paper. You will have to go over some lines more than once to keep from lifting your pencil off the paper.

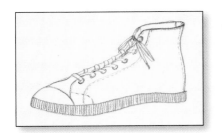

Now try making a contour drawing of another object, such as a shoe. Look at your paper and lift your pencil whenever you want to. Then add details.

TONAL DRAWING

Tonal drawings show the dark and light areas of objects using tones, or shades, of one color. They do not include contour lines. Look at the photograph at the right. Notice which areas are dark and which are light. Now look at the tonal drawing. Even without contour lines, you can tell what the drawing shows. ▶

◀ **Experiment with your pencils.** You can use **cross-hatching,** or a pattern of crossed lines, to show dark areas in a tonal drawing. Try smudging some of the lines together with your fingers. To darken large areas, use the flat edge of a dull pencil point. Use an eraser to lighten some of your marks.

Try a tonal drawing of a simple object ▶ **like a spoon.** Look at the object closely. Do not draw contour lines. Notice the shapes of the dark and light areas on the object. Use the edge of your pencil point to copy the dark shapes. Use cross-hatching in some areas. Use an eraser to lighten marks where needed.

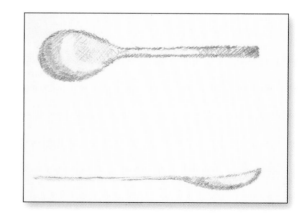

CONTOURS AND TONES

Try combining tonal drawing with contour drawing. Start by making a tonal drawing of something with an interesting shape, like a backpack. Look at it carefully to see the tones of dark and light. ▶

Then look at the object again to see its contours. Draw contour lines around the shapes that make up the object. ▶

You might prefer to start with a contour drawing. Be sure you draw the outline of each shape in the object. Then add tones with shading or cross-hatching. ▼

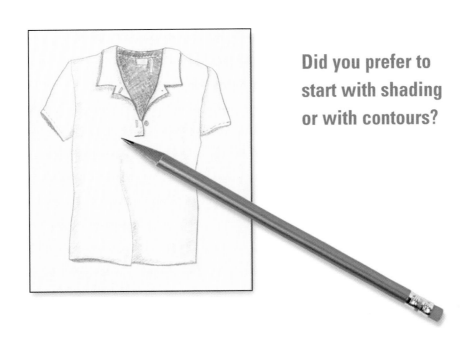

Did you prefer to start with shading or with contours?

153

Art Techniques

Experimenting with Paint

Working with colors is always fun. Experimenting with paint will help you learn about color and how you can use it in your artwork.

These are some things you should have when you paint: old newspapers to cover your work area, an old shirt to cover your clothes, tempera paints or watercolors, plastic plates or plastic egg cartons for mixing paint, paper, paintbrushes, a jar or bowl of water, and paper towels.

TEMPERA PAINTS

Tempera paints are water-based, so they are easy to clean up. The colors are bright and easy to mix.

GETTING STARTED

Start experimenting with different kinds of brushstrokes. Try painting with lots of paint on the brush and then with the brush almost dry. (You can dry the paintbrush by wiping it across a paper towel.) Make a brushstroke by twisting the paintbrush on your paper. See how many different brushstrokes you can make by rolling, pressing, or dabbing the brush on the paper.

Now load your brush with as much paint as it will ▶ **hold, and make a heavy brushstroke.** Use a craft stick or another tool to draw a pattern in it.

Use what you've learned to paint a picture. Use as many different brushstrokes as you can. ▶

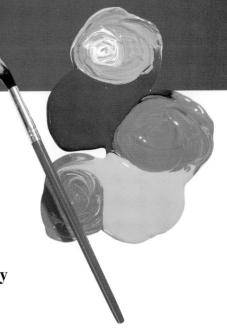

MIXING COLORS

Even if you have only a few colors of tempera paint, you can mix them to make almost any color you want. Use the **primary colors** red, yellow, and blue to create the **secondary colors** orange, green, and violet.

◀ **Mix dark and light colors.** To make darker colors (**shades**), add black. To make lighter colors (**tints**), add white. See how many shades and tints of a single color you can make.

TECHNIQUES TO TRY

Pointillism is a technique that makes the viewer's eyes mix the colors. Use colors, such as blue and yellow, that make a third color when mixed. Make small dots of color close together without letting the dots touch. In some areas, place the two different colors very close together. Stand back from your paper. What happens to the colors as your eyes "mix" them? ▶

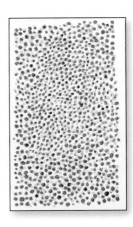

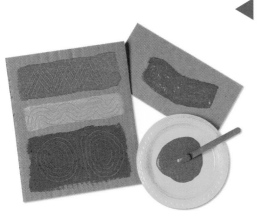

◀ **Impasto is a technique that creates a thick or bumpy surface on a painting.** You can create an impasto painting by building up layers of paint, or by thickening your paint with a material such as wheat paste. Mix some paint and wheat paste in a small bowl. Spread some of the mixture on a piece of cardboard. Experiment with tools such as a toothpick, a plastic fork, or a comb to make textures in the impasto. Mix more colors and use them to make an impasto picture or design.

Art Techniques

WATERCOLORS

Watercolors usually come in little dry cakes. You have to add the water! So keep a jar of clean water and some paper towels nearby as you paint. Use paper that is made for watercolors.

GETTING STARTED

Dip your paintbrush in water and then dab it on one of the watercolors. Try a brushstroke. Watercolors are transparent. Since you can see through them, the color on your paper will never be as dark as the color of the cake. Use different amounts of water. What happens to the color when you use a lot of water?

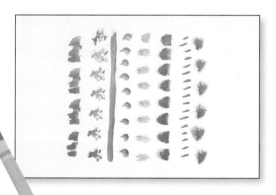

Now rinse your brush in water and use another color. Try different kinds of brushstrokes—thick and thin, squiggles and waves, dots and blobs. Change colors often.

Try using one color on top of a different color that is already dry. Work quickly. If your brushstrokes are too slow, the dry color underneath can become dull. If you want part of your painting to be white, don't paint that part. The white comes from the color of the paper.

MIXING COLORS

Experiment with mixing watercolors right on your paper. Try painting with a very wet brush. Add a wet color on top of, or just touching, another wet color. Try three colors together. ▶

You can also mix colors on your paintbrush. Dip your brush into one color and then another before you paint. Try it with green and yellow. Clean your paintbrush and try some other combinations. To clean any paint cakes that you have used for mixing, just wipe them with a paper towel. ▶

TECHNIQUES TO TRY

◀ **Try making a watercolor wash.** Start with a patch of dark green. Then clean your paintbrush and get it very wet. Use it to "wash" the color down the page. (You can also do this with a foam brush or a sponge.)

You can wet all of one side of the paper, brush a stroke of color across it, and let the color spread. Try two or three color washes together. For a special effect, sprinkle salt onto the wet paper.

Try using tempera paints and watercolors together. ▶ Start with a two-color watercolor wash. Let it dry. Then use several kinds of brushstrokes to paint a design on top of the wash with tempera paint.

Remember these techniques when you paint designs or pictures. Be sure to clean your paintbrushes and work area when you have finished.

Art Techniques

Working with Clay

Clay is a special kind of mud or earth that holds together and is easy to shape when it is mixed with water. Clay objects can be fired, or heated at a high temperature, to make them harden. They can also be left in the air to dry until hard.

To make an object with clay, work on a clean, dry surface. (A brown paper bag makes a good work surface.) Have some water handy. If the clay starts to dry out, add a few drops of water at a time. When you are not working with the clay, store it in a plastic bag to keep it moist.

▲ **You can use an assortment of tools.** Use a rolling pin to make flat slabs of clay. Use a plastic knife or fork, keys, a comb, or a pencil to add texture or designs to the objects you make out of clay.

▲ **Start working with a piece of clay by making sure it has no air bubbles in it.** Press it down, fold it over, and press it down again. This process is called **kneading**.

MODELING

Try making different forms with your clay. If one of your forms reminds you of an animal or a person, continue to mold the form by pinching and pulling the clay.

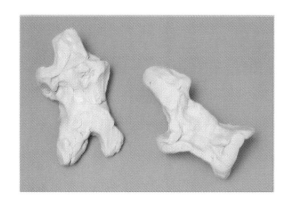

You can join two pieces of clay together. Carve small lines on the edges that will be joined. This is called **scoring**. Then use **slip,** or clay dissolved in water, to wet the surfaces. Press the pieces together and smooth the seams.

To make a bigger form, wrap a slab of clay around a tube or crumpled newspaper.

Try adding patterns, textures, or details to your form. Experiment with your tools. Press textured objects into the clay and lift them off. Brush a key across the clay. Press textured material like burlap into your clay, lift it off, and add designs. If you change your mind, smooth the clay with your fingers and try something else.

Art Techniques

USING SLABS

Roll your clay out flat, to between $\frac{1}{4}$ inch and $\frac{1}{2}$ inch thick. Shape the clay by molding it over something like a bowl or crumpled paper. ▶

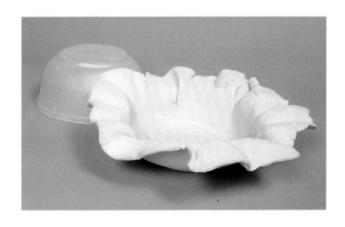

◀ **To make a slab box, roll your clay out flat.** Use a plastic knife to cut six equal-sized squares or rectangles for the bottom, top, and sides of your box. Score the edges, and then let the pieces dry until they feel like leather.

Join the pieces together with slip. ▶ Then smooth the seams with your fingers.

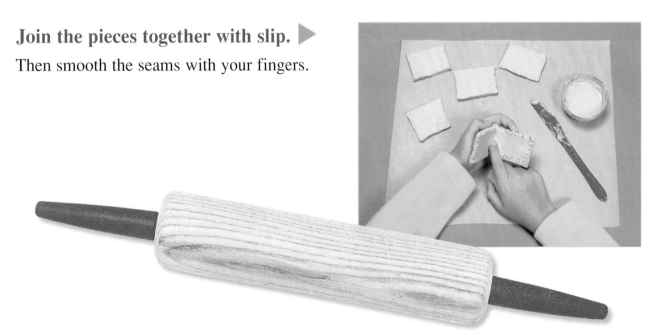

USING COILS

To make a coil pot, roll pieces of clay against a hard surface. Use your whole hand to make long clay ropes. ▶

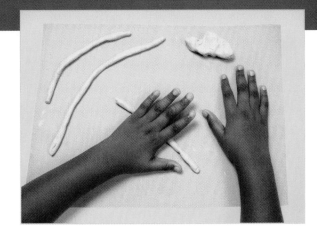

◀ **Make the bottom of your pot by curling a clay rope into a circle.** Smooth the seams with your fingers. To build the sides, attach coils of clay on top of one another. Score and wet the pieces with slip as you attach them. Smooth the inside as you work. You may smooth the outside or let the coils show.

MAKING A CLAY RELIEF ▶

A relief is a sculpture raised from a surface. To make a relief, draw a simple design on a slab of clay. Roll some very thin ropes and attach them to the lines of the design. This is called the **additive method** because you are adding clay to the slab.

◀ **You can also make a relief sculpture by carving a design out of your clay slab.** This is called the **subtractive method** because you are taking away, or subtracting, clay from the slab.

Art Techniques

Exploring Printmaking

When you make a print, you transfer color from one object to another. If you have ever left a muddy footprint on a clean floor, you know what a print is. Here are some printmaking ideas to try.

COLLOGRAPH PRINTS

A **collograph** is a combination of a **collage** and a **print**. To make a collograph, you will need cardboard, glue, paper, newspapers, a brayer (a roller for printing), printing ink or paint, a flat tray such as a foam food tray, and some paper towels or sponges. You will also need some flat objects to include in the collage. Try things like old keys, string, lace, paper clips, buttons, small shells, or burlap.

Arrange objects on the cardboard ▶ **in a pleasing design.** Glue the objects to the surface, and let the glue dry.

Prepare your ink while the collage ▶ **is drying.** Place a small amount of ink or paint on your foam tray. Roll the brayer through the ink until it is evenly coated. Gently run the brayer over the collage. Most of the ink should be on the objects.

Now press a piece of paper onto ▶ **the inked collage.** Gently rub the paper. Peel off the paper and let the ink dry. You've made a collograph!

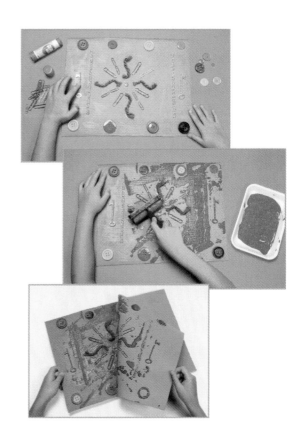

MULTICOLOR PRINTS

You can use different colors of tempera paint to make a multicolor print with repeated shapes. You will need poster board or a foam tray (such as a food tray), cardboard, scissors, glue, paper, water, tempera paint, and a paintbrush.

First cut out some interesting shapes from the poster board or foam tray. Carve or poke holes and lines into the shapes. ▶

Arrange the shapes on the cardboard to make an interesting design. Glue down the pieces. When the glue is dry, paint the shapes with different colors of tempera paint. Try not to get paint on the cardboard. ▶

◀ **While the paint is wet, place a sheet of paper on top of your design.** Gently rub the paper, and peel it off carefully. Let the paint dry.

After the shapes dry, paint them again with different colors. Print the same paper again, but turn it so that the designs and colors overlap.

Try using different colors, paper, and objects to make prints.

Art Techniques

Displaying Your Artwork

Displaying your artwork is a good way to share it.
Here are some ways to make your artwork look its best.

DISPLAYING ART PRINTS

Select several pictures that go together well. Line them up along a wall or on the floor. Try grouping the pictures in different ways. Choose an arrangement that you like. Attach a strong string across a wall. Use clothespins or paper clips to hang your pictures on the string.

Make a frame. Use a piece of cardboard that is longer and wider than the art. In the center of the cardboard, draw a rectangle that is slightly smaller than your picture. Have an adult help you cut out the rectangle. Then decorate your frame. Choose colors and textures that look good with your picture. You can paint the frame or use a stamp to print a design on it. You can add texture by gluing strips of cardboard or rows of buttons onto your frame.

Mount your picture. Tape the corners of your artwork to the back of the frame. Cut a solid piece of cardboard the same size as the frame. Then glue the framed artwork to the cardboard. Tape a loop of thread on the back. Hang up your framed work.

DISPLAYING SCULPTURES

To display your clay objects or sculptures, find a location where your work will be safe from harm. Look for a display area where people won't bump into your exhibit or damage your work.

Select several clay objects or sculptures that go together well. Try grouping them in different ways. Place some of the smaller objects on boxes. When you find an arrangement that you like, remove your artworks, tape the boxes to the table, and drape a piece of cloth over the boxes. Pick a plain cloth that will look good under your artworks, try adding a few interesting folds in the cloth, and place your artworks back on the table.

Now invite your friends and family over to see your work!

165

Line

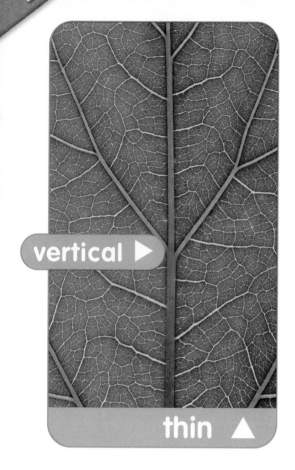

vertical ▶

thin ▲

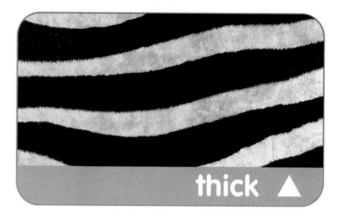

thick ▲

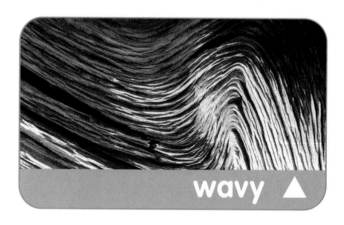

wavy ▲

straight ▼

horizontal ▲

zigzag ▼

Shape

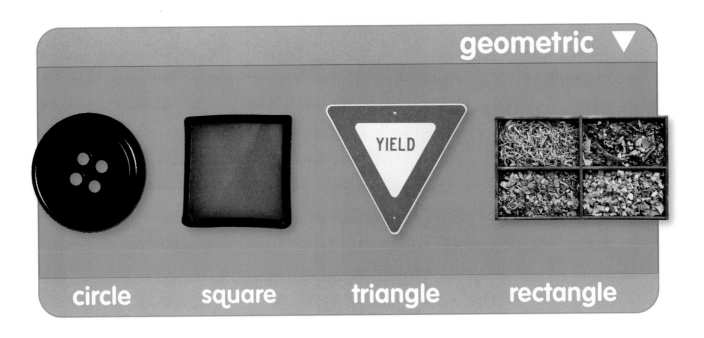

geometric ▼

circle   square   triangle   rectangle

symbol ▲

▼ organic

Color and Value

color wheel ▲

cool colors ▲

warm colors ▲

complementary colors ▲

▼ value

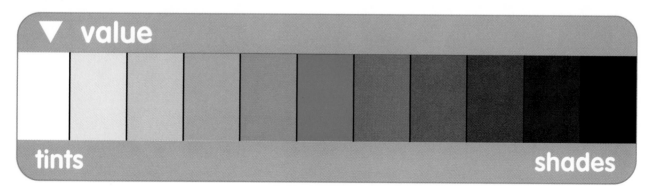

tints

shades

bumpy ▲

▼ soft

silky ▲

rough ▲

▼ smooth

169

Form

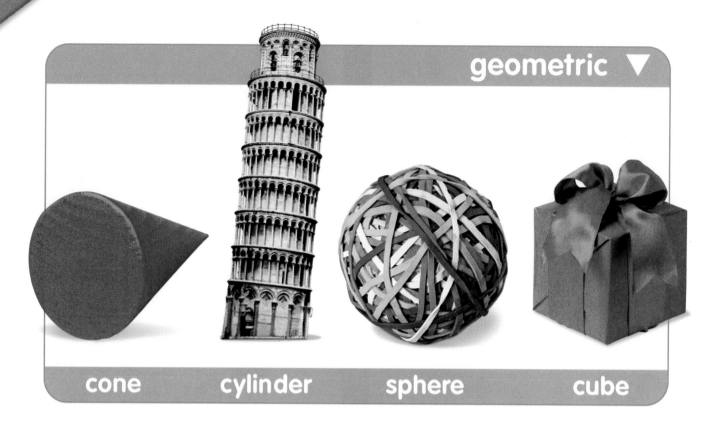

geometric ▼

cone   cylinder   sphere   cube

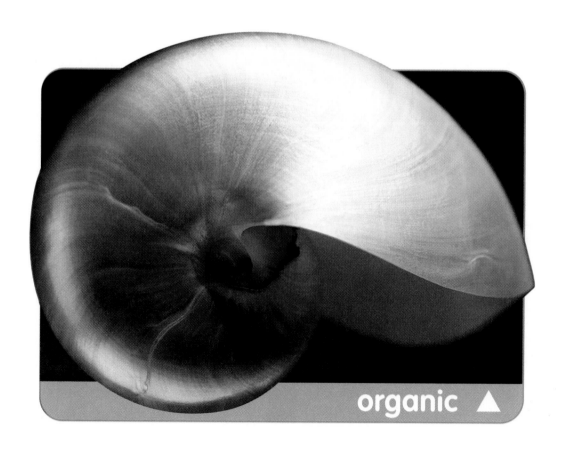

organic ▲

Space

overlapping ▼

atmospheric perspective ▼

background ▶

middle ground ▶

foreground ▶

positive ▶

◀ negative

▲ **linear perspective**

Pattern

Proportion

Balance

▼ radial

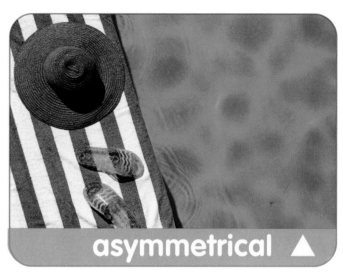

asymmetrical ▲

symmetrical ▲

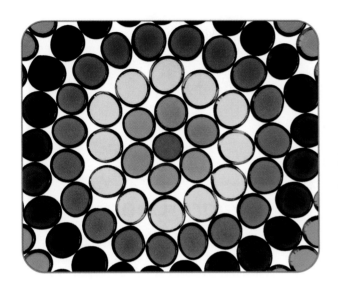

Gallery of Artists

Alexander Archipenko
(1887–1964) page 38

Romare Bearden
(1911–1988) pages 116 and 117

Emil Armin
(1883–1971) page 28

Charles Bell
(1935–1995) page 58

Jennifer Bartlett
(1941–) page 106

Thomas Hart Benton
(1889–1975) page 44

Carl Oscar Borg
(1879–1947) page 91

Dale Chihuly
(1941–) page 38

Fernando Botero
(1932–) page 34

Christo
(1935–) page 99

Alexander Calder
(1898–1976) page 104

Clarice Cliff
(1899–1972) page 126

Gallery of Artists

Robert Delaunay

(1885–1941) page 46

Robert S. Duncanson

(1821–1872) page 87

Sonia Delaunay

(1885–1979) page 114

Louise Freshman-Brown

page 132

Arthur G. Dove

(1880–1946) page 61

Frank O. Gehry

(1929–) page 131

180

Arturo Gordon

(1883–1944) page 86

Jack Gunter

page 59

Juan Gris

(1887–1927) page 112

Barbara Hepworth

(1903–1975) page 37

Red Grooms

(1937–) page 92

Ando Hiroshige

(1797–1858) page 88

Winslow Homer

(1836–1910) pages 96 and 97

Edward Hopper

(1882–1967) page 82

Jeanne-Claude

(1935–) page 99

Nicario Jimenez

pages 136 and 137

William H. Johnson

(1901–1970) page 35

Frida Kahlo

(1907–1954) page 66

Wassily Kandinsky

(1866–1944) pages 30 and 31

Kasimir Malevich

(1878–1935) page 121

Paul Klee

(1879–1940) page 102

Henri Matisse

(1869–1954) pages 22 and 26

Johanna Kriesel

page 139

John Gaw Meem

(1894–1983) page 130

Reynard Milici

(1942–) page 94

Henry Moore

(1898–1986) pages 70 and 71

Joan Miró

(1893–1983) page 41

Bartolomé E. Murillo

(1618–1682) page 24

Claude Monet

(1840–1926) page 84

Louise Nevelson

(1899–1988) page 134

Georgia O'Keeffe

(1887–1986) page 48

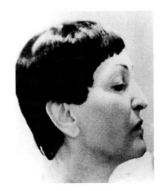

Meret Oppenheim

(1913–1985) page 54

Claes Oldenburg

(1929–) page 42

Pablo Picasso

(1881–1973) page 108

Diana Ong

(1940–) page 36

Patricia Polacco

(1944–) page 111

Edward Potthast

(1857–1927) page 68

Henri Rousseau

(1844–1910) page 66

Pierre-Auguste Renoir

(1841–1919) page 62

Beatricia Sagar

page 128

Diego Rivera

(1886–1957) pages 52 and 78

Kurt Schwitters

(1887–1948) page 119

David Stewart

(1939–) page 134

Josephine Trotter

page 49

Harriet Peck Taylor

(1954–) page 64

Patssi Valdez

page 107

Alma Woodsey Thomas

(1891–1978) pages 50 and 51

Coosje van Bruggen

(1942–) page 42

Gallery of Artists

Vincent van Gogh
(1853–1890) page 101

Andy Warhol
(1928–1987) page 141

Anna Belle Lee Washington
(1924–2000) page 124

Tom Wesselmann
(1931–) page 118

Glossary

The Glossary contains important art terms and their definitions. Each word is respelled as it would be in a dictionary. When you see this mark ' after a syllable, pronounce that syllable with more force than the other syllables.

a add	e end	o odd	o͞o pool	oi oil	t͟h this		a in above
ā ace	ē equal	ō open	u up	ou pout	zh vision	ə =	e in sicken
â care	i it	ô order	û burn	ng ring			i in possible
ä palm	ī ice	o͝o took	yo͞o fuse	th thin			o in melon
							u in circus

A

abstract art [ab′strakt ärt]
Art that does not look realistic. Abstract art may show either distorted objects or no real objects at all. (page 112)

artist [är′tist] A person who makes art. (page 12)

artwork [ärt′wûrk] A work of art, such as a drawing, painting, or sculpture. (page 14)

assemblage [ə•sem′blij]
A sculpture made of different kinds of materials. (page 134)

asymmetrical balance
[ā•sə•me′tri•kəl ba′ləns] A kind of balance in which different lines, shapes, and colors are used on each side of an artwork to make both sides seem equal. (page 108) (*See also* symmetrical balance.)

B

background [bak′ground]
The part of an artwork that seems to be farthest away from the viewer. (page 88)

background

center of interest

[sen′tər əv in′trəst] The part of an artwork that the viewer notices first. (page 94)

cityscape [si′tē•skāp] An artwork that shows a view of a city. (page 92)

collage [kə•läzh′] An artwork made by gluing bits of paper, fabric, scraps, photographs, or other materials to a flat surface. (page 118)

complementary colors

[kom•plə•men′tər•ē kul′ərz] Pairs of colors that are opposite each other on the color wheel. (page 114)

complementary colors

composition [kom•pə•zish′ən] The way the parts of an artwork are put together. (page 34)

contour line [kon′toor līn] An outline drawn around a shape or an object. (page 27)

contrast [kän′trast] A difference between two parts of an artwork that makes one or both stand out. (page 94)

cool colors [kool kul′ərz] The colors green, blue, and violet. These colors appear on one half of the color wheel. (page 49) (*See also* warm colors.)

cool colors

depth [depth] The appearance of space or distance in a two-dimensional artwork. (page 86)

distortion [dis•tôr′shən] The changing of the way an object looks by bending or stretching its shape. (page 112)

earthwork [ûrth•wûrk] A kind of art that is made of natural materials and placed in a natural setting. Also called *land art* or *environmental art*. (page 98)

emphasis [em′fə•sis] A design principle used to show which part of an artwork is most important. (page 94)

foreground [fôr′ground] The part of an artwork that seems to be closest to the viewer. (page 88)

foreground

form [fôrm] An object that has height, width, and depth. Forms can be geometric or organic. (page 38)

forms

found object [found ob′jikt] An everyday object used as part of an artwork. (page 134)

geometric shape
[jē•ə•met′rik shāp] A shape, such as an oval, circle, square, triangle, or rectangle, that has a regular outline. (page 32) (*See also* organic shape.)

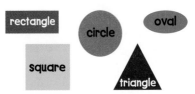

rectangle
circle
oval
square
triangle

graphic arts [graf′ik ärts] A kind of artwork that can be used over and over in advertisements and signs. (page 138)

grid [grid] A pattern of squares of equal size. (page 106)

horizon line [hə•rī′zən līn] A line in the distance where the sky seems to meet land or water. (page 86)

image [im′ij] A picture of an artwork. (page 24)

intermediate colors [in•tər•mē′dē•ət kul′ərz] Colors that are created by mixing a primary color with a secondary color. (page 47)

primary   secondary   intermediate
color   color   color

jagged line [jag′id līn] A line that is uneven or ragged. (page 28)

landscape [land′skāp] An artwork that shows an outdoor scene. (page 28)

line [līn] A mark that begins at one point and continues for a certain distance in a certain direction. (page 26)

mola [mō′lə] An artwork made by sewing together layers of brightly colored cloth. (page 74)

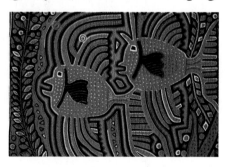

movement [mōōv′mənt] A design principle used to guide the viewer's eye around an artwork. (page 69)

mural [myŏŏr′əl] A very large painting that covers a wall. (page 78)

neutral colors [nōō′trəl kul′ərz] Colors, such as brown or gray, that can be created by mixing two complementary colors. (page 114)

object [ob′jikt] Something that takes up space and can be seen or touched. (page 26)

organic shape [ôr•gan′ik shāp] A shape with irregular borders, like shapes that appear in nature. (page 32) (*See also* geometric shape.)

organic shapes

overlapping [ō•vər•lap′ing] The placement of some objects to partly cover other objects. Artists use overlapping to show which objects are closest to the viewer. (page 92)

painting [pān′ting] A two-dimensional artwork made with paint. (page 26)

pattern [pa′tərn] A design made up of repeated lines, shapes, or colors. (page 72)

photomontage [fō•tō•mon•täzh′] An artwork made of cut or torn photographs. (page 132)

photorealism [fō•tō•rē′əl•iz•əm] A style of painting that looks almost like a photograph. (page 58)

portrait [pôr′trət] A picture that shows what a person, a group of people, or an animal looks like. (page 66)

primary colors [prī′mer•ē kul′ərz] The colors red, yellow, and blue. They are mixed together to make other colors on the color wheel. (page 46)

print [print] An artwork made by pressing an object covered with wet color against a flat surface. (page 128)

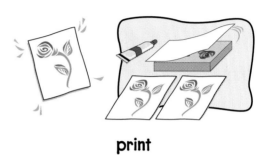

print

proportion [prə•pôr′shən] The size and placement of one thing compared with the size and placement of other things. (page 66)

rhythm [ri′thəm] The visual beat created by repeated lines, shapes, colors, or patterns in an artwork. (page 128)

scene [sēn] A view of a certain place. (page 28)

sculpture [skulp′chər] A three-dimensional artwork. (page 38)

seascape [sē′skāp] An artwork that shows a view of an ocean or a sea. (page 68)

secondary colors [se′kən•der•ē kul′ərz] The colors orange, green, and violet. Each one is created by combining two primary colors. (page 47)

self-portrait [self•pôr′trət] A portrait of an artist made by himself or herself. (page 66)

shade [shād] A darker value of a color made by mixing it with black. (page 52) (*See also* tint.)

sketch [skech] A rough or unfinished drawing that often shows a plan for an artwork. (page 12)

space [spās] The distance or area between or around objects. (page 86)

still life [stil līf] An artwork that shows a group of objects placed together in an interesting way. (page 34)

symbol [sim′bəl] A picture or object that stands for an idea. (page 126)

symmetrical balance

[sə•me′tri•kəl ba′ləns] A kind of balance in which the same lines, shapes, and colors are placed on both sides of an artwork. (page 106) (*See also* asymmetrical balance.)

symmetry [sim′ə•trē] An arrangement in which one half of an artwork is a mirror image of the other half. (page 72)

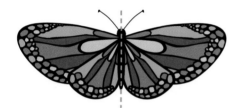

tactile texture

[tak′təl teks′chər] The way a surface of a real object feels when you touch it. *Smooth, rough,* and *furry* are words that describe tactile textures. (page 54)

three-dimensional

[thrē•də•men′shə•nəl] Having height, width, and depth. (page 38) (*See also* two-dimensional.)

tint [tint] A lighter value of a color made by mixing it with white. (page 52) (*See also* shade.)

two-dimensional

[too•də•men′shə•nəl] Having height and width; flat. (page 32) (*See also* three-dimensional.)

unity [yoo′nə•tē] The sense that an artwork looks whole or complete. (page 114)

value [val′yoo] The lightness or darkness of a color. (page 52)

variety [və•rī′ə•tē] A design
principle used to add interest
to an artwork by including
different objects and art
elements. (page 126)

visual texture
[vizh′oo•əl teks′chər] Drawn or
painted texture that looks like
real textures. (page 58)

warm colors [wärm kul′ərz]
The colors red, orange, and
yellow. These colors appear
on one half of the color wheel.
(page 48) (*See also* cool
colors.)

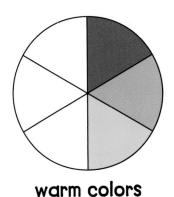

warm colors

weaving [wēv′ing] An artwork
made by lacing together fibers
such as yarn, thread, or strips
of fabric. Rugs and baskets are
kinds of weavings. (page 54)

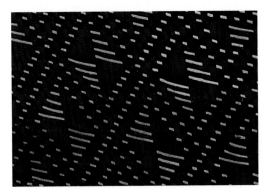

Index of Artists and Artworks

Index

Index

Acknowledgments

Photo Credits:

Page Placement Key: (t)-top (c)-center (b)-bottom (l)-left (r)-right (fg)-foreground (bg)-background.

All photos property of Harcourt except for the following:

Frontmatter:

5 (tl) Erich Lessing/Art Resource, NY; (tc) Louis K. Meisel Gallery/Corbis; 6 (tl) Indigo Arts Gallery; (tr) Superstock; (tc) Reprinted with the permission of Simon & Shuster Books for Young Readers, an imprint of Simon & Schuster Children's Publishing Division from COYOTE PLACES THE STARS by Harriet Peck Taylor; 7 (tr) Laura Atkins; (tc) Michael Boys/Corbis; 8 (tc) Artist Rights Society (ARS), New York, NY/National Museum of Modern Art, Paris, France/Lauros-Giraudon, Paris/Superstock ; 9 (tl) Tanaya2/May Lee Clark Elementary School ; 14 (tr) Bob Kirst/Corbis; (bl) F. Carter Smith/Corbis Sygma; 15 (bl) Royalty-Free/Corbis; 16 (b) Josephine Trotter/Superstock; 17 (b) Artist Rights Society (ARS), New York, NY/Los Angeles County Museum of Art, Gift of Mr. and Mrs. Milton W. Lipper from the Milton W. Lipper Fund; 21 (tl) Alamy Images; (tr) Alamy Images.

Unit 1:

22 (t) Artist Rights Society (ARS), New York, NY/Erich Lessing/Art Resource, NY; 23 (bl) AKG Images; 24 (b) National Gallery of Art, Washington D.C.; 26 (c) Artist Rights Society (ARS), New York, NY/CNAC/MNAM/Dist. Reunion des Musees Nationaux/Art Resource, NY; 28 (c) Smithsonian American Art Museum, Washington, DC/Art Resource, NY; 30 (t) Artist Rights Society (ARS), New York, NY/CNAC/NMAM/Dist. Reunion des Musees Nationaux/Art Resource, NY; (b) Bettmann/Corbis; 31 (b) Erich Lessing/Art Resource, NY; (t) Artist Rights Society (ARS), New York, NY/Christie's Images/Superstock; 32 (cl) Joseph Barnell/Superstock; 34 (b) Christie's Images/Corbis; 35 (tl) Smithsonian American Art Museum, Washington, DC/Art Resource, NY; (tr) Lauren/Smiley Elementary School; 36 (b) Artist Rights Society (ARS), New York, NY/Diana Ong/Superstock; 37 (b) Licensed by VAGA, New York, NY/Alan Bowness, Hepworth Estate/Tate; 38 (br) Dale Chihuly; (bl) Artist Rights Society (ARS), New York/Solomon R. Guggenheim Museum; 41 (cr) Solomon R. Guggenheim Museum.

Unit 2:

42 (t) University of Nebraska-Lincoln, Olga N. Sheldon Acquisition Trust and friends of Sheldon Memorial Art Gallery; 43 (bl) AP/Wide World Photos; (bl) Thomas Hoepker/Magnum Photos; 44 (b) (copyright) T.H. Benton and R.P. Benton Testamentary Trusts/Licensed by VAGA, New York, NY/Hunter Museum of American Art, Chattanooga, Tennessee, Gift of the Benwood Foundation; 46 (b) Giraudon/Art Resource, NY; 48 (b) Artist Rights Society (ARS), New York, NY/New Orleans Museum of Art: Museum purchase, City of New Orleans Capital Funds; 49 (tr) Josephine Trotter/Superstock; 50 (br) Licensed by VAGA, New York, NY/Smithsonian American Art Museum, Washington, DC/Art Resource, NY; (t) Smithsonian American Art Museum, Washington, DC/Art Resource, NY; 51 (t) Licensed by VAGA, New York,NY/Smithsonian American Art Museum, Washington, DC/Art Resource, NY; 52 (b) Los Angeles County Museum of Art, Gift of Mr. and Mrs. Milton W. Lipper from the Milton W. Lipper Fund; 54 (b) Artist Rights Society (ARS), New York, NY/Digital Image (c) The Museum of Modern Art/Licensed by SCALA/Art Resource, NY; 56 (b) Swift/Vanuga Images/Corbis; 57 (b) Kelly-Mooney Photography/Corbis; (t) Massimo Mastrorillo/Corbis; 58 (b) Louis K. Meisel Gallery/Corbis ; 59 (t) Jack Gunter/Corbis; 61 (bl) Butler Institute of American Art.

Unit 3:

62 (t) National Gallery, Berlin/Superstock; 63 (bl) Francis G. Mayer/Corbis; 64 (t, b) Artist Rights Society (ARS), New York, NY/Simon & Schuster Publishing; 66 (bl) Schalkwijk/Art Resource, NY; (br) Art Resource, NY; 68 (c) Superstock; 70 (b) Francis G. Mayer/Corbis; 71 (cr) John Swope Collection/Corbis; (t) Henry Moore Foundation/Scala/Art Resource, NY; 72 (bl) Peabody Museum of Archeology and Ethnology; (br) Indigo Arts Gallery; 74 (b) Gift of Mrs. H. Lester Cooke/Textile Museum; 76 (b) National Archives and Records Administration; 77 (t) Richard Cummins/Corbis; (b) Hannah Goodwin/Harcourt; (c) Danny Lehman/Corbis; 78 (b) Schalkwijk/Art Resource, NY; 79 (t) Ms. Filis; 81 (c) Royalty-Free/Corbis.

Unit 4:

82(t) Francis G. Mayer/Corbis; 83 (bl) Copyright National Portrait Gallery, Smithsonian Institution/Art Resource, NY; 84 (b) Alfred Atmore Pope Collection, Hill-Stead Museum, Farmington CT; (tl) The Shelburne Museum; 86 (b) Kactus Foto/Superstock; 87 (tl) Smithsonian American Art Museum, Washington, DC/Art Resource, NY; 88 (bl) The Newark Museum/Art Resource, NY; 90 (l) Royalty-Free/Corbis; 91 (l) Smithsonian American Art Museum, Washington, DC/Art Resource, NY; 92 (l) Artist Rights Society (ARS), New York, NY/Red Grooms, b. 1937. *Looking Along Broadway Towards Grace Church, 1981. Mixed media, H. 180.3 cm. Image (copyright)* The Cleveland Museum of Art, gift of Agnes Gund in honor of Edward Henning, 1991.27; 93 (t) Laura Atkins; 94 (bl) Louis K. Meisel Gallery/Corbis; 96 (b) Burstein Collection/Corbis; (tl) Bettmann/Corbis; 97 (t) Indianapolis Museum of Art, Martha Delzell Memorial Fund; 98 (b) Michael Boys/Corbis; 99 (tl) Christo and Jeanne Claude; 101 (br) Art Resource, NY.

Unit 5:

102 (t) Artist Rights Society (ARS), New York, NY/Francis G. Mayer/Corbis; 103 (bl) Hulton Archive/Getty Images; 104 (b) Art Resource, NY; 106 (b) Geoffrey Clements/Corbis; 107 (t) Patssi Valdez/Patricia Correia Gallery; 108 (bl) Artist Rights Society (ARS), New York, NY/Giraudon/Art Resource, NY; 110 (t) From APPELEMANDO'S DREAM by Patricia Polacco, copyright (c) 1991 by Patricia Polacco. Used by permission of Philomel Books, A Division of Penguin Young Readers Group, A Member of Penguin Group (USA) Inc., 345 Hudson Street, New York, NY 10014. All rights reserved.; 110-111 (b) Patricia Polacco ; 111 (t) From APPELEMANDO'S DREAM by Patricia Polacco, copyright (c) 1991 by Patricia Polacco. Used by permission of Philomel Books, A Division of Penguin Young Readers Group, A Member of Penguin Group (USA) Inc., 345 Hudson Street, New York, NY 10014. All